NEW TESTAMENT

WORDS

for Today

100 Devotional Reflections

WARREN W. WIERSBE

BakerBooks

a division of Baker Publishing Group
Grand Rapids, Michigan

© 2013 by Warren W. Wiersbe

Published by Baker Books
a division of Baker Publishing Group
P.O. Box 6287, Grand Rapids, MI 49516-6287
www.bakerbooks.com

Printed in the United States of America

Library of Congress Cataloging-in-Publication Data
Wiersbe, Warren W.
    New Testament words for today : 100 devotional reflections / Warren W. Wiersbe
        pages cm
    ISBN 978-0-8010-1577-9 (pbk.)
    1. Bible. New Testament—Meditations. I. Title.
BS2341.55.W54 2013
242'.5—dc23   2013017835

In keeping with biblical principles of creation stewardship, Baker Publishing Group advocates the responsible use of our natural resources. As a member of the Green Press Initiative, our company uses recycled paper when possible. The text paper of this book is composed in part of post-consumer waste.

green press INITIATIVE

13   14   15   16   17   18   19   7   6   5   4   3   2   1

Preface

Yet in the church I would rather speak *five words
with my understanding*, that I may teach others
also, than ten thousand words in a tongue.

══════════════ 1 CORINTHIANS 14:19

If you know how to select them, five words can express
unforgettable, life-changing thoughts.

Thomas Jefferson put five words into the Declaration of
Independence that declared liberty for the American colonies:
"We hold these truths to be self-evident, that *all men are
created equal*." Abraham Lincoln quoted those five words
in his famous Gettysburg Address.

"*A specter is haunting Europe*" are the words Karl Marx and
Friedrich Engels chose to open their *Communist Manifesto*,
a small book whose message changed the map of Europe.

On June 18, 1940, Prime Minister Winston Churchill heart-
ened the British people with a speech that concluded with five
unforgettable words: "Let us therefore brace ourselves to our
duty, and so bear ourselves that, if the British Commonwealth

and its Empire lasts for a thousand years, men will still say, '*This was their finest hour.*'"

The Bible contains many memorable five-word statements that are "living and powerful" (Heb. 4:12), inspired words that the Holy Spirit can use to direct us in today's chaotic world. In this book, I have provided meditations based on one hundred of these phrases as they are found in the New Testament, using the New King James Version of the Scriptures.

I trust that as you meditate on God's Word and ponder my words, the Spirit of God will enlighten you and encourage you, enabling you to discover the will of God and enjoy doing it.

Warren W. Wiersbe

NEW
TESTAMENT
WORDS
for Today

1

And [Joseph] did not know [Mary] till she had brought forth her firstborn Son. And *he called His name Jesus.*

MATTHEW 1:25

The Lord is not in a hurry. For centuries, God had led different people in different places to do different things to prepare the way for the birth of Jesus in Bethlehem, and now he had come. "But when the fullness of the time had come, God sent forth His Son" (Gal. 4:4). In Malachi 1:11, God had promised that his name would be "great among the nations," and now the one had arrived who would fulfill that promise (John 17:4). His is the first name and the last name in the New Testament (Matt. 1:1; Rev. 22:21); and between those verses, the name of Jesus is mentioned over nine hundred times. In the first chapter of Matthew, the name *Jesus* is linked with two other names: *Christ* and *Immanuel*. His official name is *Christ*, which means "anointed" and reminds us that Jesus is prophet, priest, and king. In the Hebrew nation, the men in these offices were always anointed with special oil. *Immanuel* means "God with us," reminding us that Jesus is God and is always present with his people. *Jesus* is his personal name, and it means "Savior." Let's think about that name.

Jesus *is a divinely appointed name.* The angel who visited Mary told her to call her son Jesus (Luke 1:31); and in his dream Joseph saw an angel who gave him the same command (Matt. 1:21), which he obeyed (v. 25). When the baby was circumcised, Jesus was the name given to him (Luke 2:21). The name *Jesus* comes from the Hebrew *Yehoshua* (Joshua), which means "the Lord saves." The phrase "He will save His people" in Matthew 1:21 does not refer only to the salvation of Jewish people but to that of all those who put their trust in Jesus.

Jesus *is an honorable name.* It belonged to Hoshea, one of the twelve spies, but Moses changed it to *Joshua* (Num. 13:8, 16). During the wilderness march, Joshua had been Moses's special assistant and the general of the army, but God made him Moses's successor and he led the nation into the Promised Land. But the name *Joshua* also belonged to the high priest who served the Jewish remnant that went to the Holy Land after the exile in Babylon (Hag. 1:1). Because of the prominence of these two men, a general and a high priest, many Jewish boys were named Joshua, which in the Greek language is *Jesus.*

Jesus *is an effective name.* What good news that Jesus is the Savior of lost sinners! "Nor is there salvation in any other, for there is no other name under heaven given among men by which we must be saved" (Acts 4:12). But there is more. He is the master and friend of *saved* sinners! His people have the privilege of prayer because of the authority of his name. "And whatever you ask in My name, that will I do, that the Father may be glorified in the Son. If you ask anything in My name, I will do it" (John 14:13–14). In his name we have the authority to proclaim the gospel (Luke 24:47), the opportunity to assemble with other believers and worship (Matt. 18:20), and the privilege to suffer for his name's sake (Acts 5:41; 1 Pet. 4:14).

Jesus *is an abused name.* People use his name as a swear word or else they use a "minced oath," such as "gee" or "jeeze." (Other minced oaths are "golly" and "gosh" and "jiminy crickets.") But it's up to us as God's children to magnify the name of Jesus by our good works, our godly walk, and our gracious speech.

> Therefore God also has highly exalted Him and given Him the name which is above every name, that at the name of Jesus every knee should bow, of those in heaven, and of those on earth, and of those under the earth.
>
> Philippians 2:9–10

2

And when [the magi] had come into the house,
they saw the young Child with Mary His mother,
and *fell down and worshiped Him*.

MATTHEW 2:11

In spite of what we sing during the Christmas season, the oriental magi were not kings but rather interpreters of the stars and of dreams, and we don't know how many there were. God directed them via the star to the house in Bethlehem where the holy family was living. Consider some of the factors involved in this important event.

Persistence. We don't know which country they came from, although many students believe it was Persia. Undoubtedly there was a large train of people and animals, enough to stir Jerusalem and frighten King Herod. Travel was slow in those days, and the larger the train, the longer it took to reach the destination. Some students believe they had been traveling for perhaps a year. God's people today may have instant contact with the Savior at his throne of grace, and we know he is always with us (Matt. 28:18–20; Heb. 13:5). But it takes grace and persistence to live the Christian life. Hebrews 6:12 admonishes us not to "become sluggish, but imitate those who through faith and patience inherit the promises."

Guidance. There is no sense traveling if you don't know where you are going, but the Lord gave them guidance through a special star. Being men who searched the heavens, the magi found the star a perfect guide. But when they reached Jerusalem, the priests gave them directions to Bethlehem from Micah 5:2, and then in Bethlehem the star reappeared and took them right to the correct house. We follow the Lord's leading a step at a time. God didn't send the magi a map; he guided them day by day and they arrived at their appointed destination. God can use circumstances, other people, and his Word to point the way he wants us to go, and they will always agree. Beware of ignoring the Bible! If we spend time daily in the Scriptures, God will give us just the promise, warning, or command we need at that time.

Eminence. The magi were important and wealthy men, while most Christians are ordinary people living ordinary lives, *but all have the privilege of worshiping Jesus and serving him!* God is no respecter of persons and shows no partiality (Acts 10:34–35). We may not have lavish gifts to bring him, but if what we bring him is from our hearts, he will accept it and bless it. Jesus accepted the little boy's simple lunch (John 6:8–11) as well as Mary's expensive ointment (12:1–8), and both gifts brought blessing to others. It's likely that the magi's gifts gave Joseph the funds he needed for their escape to Egypt and the expenses for their life there.

Reverence. After entering the house, the magi "fell down and worshiped Him" (Matt. 2:11). These men were Gentiles and by their actions they demonstrated that the King of the Jews would provide salvation for all the nations of the world (4:15–16; 12:15–21). Our annual celebration of the birth of Christ ought to include thanksgiving for the Gift of God to the whole world. It should be a time for worship and praise, and we should give gifts to Jesus just as the magi did centuries ago.

The magi did not go back to Herod or to the priests, for they had found Jesus and needed nothing or no one else. Don't go beyond the King! Like the humble shepherds (Luke 2:20), the magi no doubt spread the good word at home that God had sent a Savior, and his name was Jesus. Let's follow their example.

> He who is the blessed and only Potentate, the King of kings and Lord of lords.
>
> 1 Timothy 6:15

3

In those days *John the Baptist came preaching* in the wilderness of Judea, and saying, "Repent, for the kingdom of heaven is at hand!"

MATTHEW 3:1–2

John the Baptist's sudden arrival on the scene startled the people and puzzled the Jewish religious leaders (John 1:14–28). If the priests had remembered what the prophets had written, they would have understood who John was and what he had come to do (Isa. 40:3–5; Mal. 3:3; 4:5–6). Jesus said that no man had ever been born who was greater than John the Baptist (Matt. 11:7–15). Certainly his message was the greatest, for he announced the imminent arrival of the promised Messiah and his kingdom, and he called the people to repent of their sins and welcome their Savior. John is certainly a good example to us of a faithful servant.

John came because he was sent by the Lord. "There was a man sent from God, whose name was John" (John 1:6). The word translated "sent" gives us our word *apostle* and means "one commissioned by the king and authorized to speak for him." John's work was to prepare the people for the ministry of Jesus. The spiritual condition of the Jewish people was at low ebb and John called them to repent of their sins and return to the Lord. Because John was a servant of the Lord, he had no fear of what men might say or do. He lived an austere life in the wilderness and was a man of prayer. He was like Elijah the prophet who bravely confronted King Ahab and the priests of Baal and won the battle (1 Kings 17–18). The only way to have authority and victory is to be sent by God and do the work he assigns to us.

John preached the message God gave him. There are several words in the New Testament for *preach*, and the one used here means "to herald an official message." Government officials today have numerous ways to communicate with citizens, but in John's day it was usually the voice of the official herald that gave the message. John was a witness to Jesus the Light (John 1:7–8), because the Jewish people were spiritually blind to the Light of the Lord that was shining. John gave his witness in the wilderness near the Jordan River because the people were wandering in a religious wilderness like the Jews in the Old Testament. But one of the most remarkable things about John the Baptist is that he did no miracles (10:40–42). His work was done through the preaching of the Word, just as ours is done today. Never underestimate the power of the preaching of God's Word.

John majored on exalting Jesus Christ. He said, "He must increase, but I must decrease" (3:30). He glorified Jesus and not himself. "For we do not preach ourselves, but Christ Jesus the Lord, and ourselves your bondservants for Jesus' sake" (2 Cor. 4:5). Jesus Christ is the living Word (John 1:1–2, 14), and John the Baptist declared that he was only a voice speaking the word (1:19–24). You hear a voice, but you can't see the sound unless you have special equipment. John was only a "burning and shining lamp" (5:35), but Jesus is the Light (1:6–9; 8:12). John announced Jesus as the bridegroom, but John was only the best man at the wedding (3:29). The angel told John's father that his son would be great (Luke 1:15), *but John saw to it that Jesus was always greater.*

As we seek to serve the Lord, let's be sure God has called us and sent us. Let's declare the message he has given us and be sure we magnify Jesus Christ. Jesus praised John because he wasn't a vacillating reed in the wind or a wealthy celebrity but a devoted servant of the Lord (Matt. 11:7–15). Can he say that about us?

That in all things He may have the preeminence.

Colossians 1:18

4

> And suddenly a voice came from heaven, say-
> ing, "*This is My beloved Son*, in whom I am well
> pleased."
>
> MATTHEW 3:17

The Father affirms his love. John the Baptist recognized Jesus when he came to the Jordan River to be baptized. Knowing that Jesus had no sins to confess, John tried to change his mind, but Jesus insisted that they obey the Father's will. Most New Testament scholars agree that New Testament baptism was by immersion, illustrating death, burial, and resurrection. The word "us" in verse 15 does not refer to Jesus and John but to the Father, Jesus, and the Holy Spirit who would "fulfill all righteousness" in the death, burial, and resurrection of the Son of God. Jesus referred to this "baptism" when he said in Luke 12:50, "But I have a baptism to be baptized with, and how distressed I am till it is accomplished!" This was the first of three occasions when the Father affirmed his love to his Son, and all three involved the cross. The second was on the Mount of Transfiguration (Matt. 17:1–7) and the third after Jesus's triumphal entry into Jerusalem (John 12:12–32). Whenever we face a "Calvary" situation, our Father assures us of his love.

Satan questions the Father's love. Immediately after his baptism, Jesus was led by the Spirit into the wilderness to be tempted by Satan (Matt. 4:1–11). Jesus fasted for forty days and nights, and when Satan saw that Jesus was at his weakest, he attacked him with three powerful offers. First, Satan referred to what the Father had spoken from heaven. "If you are the Son of God—and the Father said you are—why are you hungry? If your Father truly loves you, why does he deprive you of food?" (v. 3). In tempting us, one of Satan's stratagems is to get us to question our heavenly Father's love. Once he gets us to doubt God's love, Satan has an easy time destroying our faith, hope, and love. "Why do you have to die on the cross, Jesus? Is that the Father's love for you? Worship me and I will give you the kingdoms of the world and you won't have to suffer" (v. 9). Whenever you are tempted, *never once question the Father's love.* If Jesus is your Savior, then you are "accepted in the Beloved" (Eph. 1:6).

The Son demonstrates divine love at Calvary. "But God demonstrates His own love toward us, in that while we were still sinners, Christ died for us" (Rom. 5:8). The cross is the greatest proof of God's love. We know God loves us, not because we are healthy, wealthy, and enjoying an easy life, but because he told us so in the Scriptures. In fact, the Father loves us *just as he loves his own Son.* Jesus prayed to his Father "that the world may know that You have sent Me, and have loved them as You have loved Me" (John 17:23). As one of God's elect, you are beloved of the Father (Col. 3:12). All God's children are "brethren beloved by the Lord" (2 Thess. 2:13), no matter how much pain we feel or how uncomfortable our circumstances may be. When you doubt God's love, visit the cross.

Our love for others proves God's love for them. God reveals his love through his own people. The lost world will never believe John 3:16 if Christians don't obey 1 John 3:16—"By this we know love, because He laid down His life for us. And we also ought to lay down our lives for the brethren." And 1 John 4:11 says, "Beloved, if God so loved us, we also ought to love one another." Christians are to be channels, not reservoirs; we share God's love with others as the Holy Spirit works in and through us. "But the fruit of the Spirit is love" (Gal. 5:22). Love is not something we manufacture, like actors counterfeiting emotion onstage. Love is like fruit—alive, fragrant, nourishing, with seeds in it for more fruit.

Love never fails.

1 Corinthians 13:8

5

Therefore you shall be perfect, just as your Father in heaven is perfect.

MATTHEW 5:48

I mpossible!" is our first reaction to this verse, because that word *perfect* disturbs us as sinful human beings. It's one thing to do our best but quite something else when it comes to claiming "perfection." If we must be perfect, why is "Forgive us our trespasses" in the Lord's Prayer? Our heavenly Father wants us to aim for perfection because he cannot will anything less than the very best for his children. Here are some guidelines to help us in our quest.

The goal of the Christian life is godliness, and godliness simply means "God-likeness." On March 3, 1805, missionary Henry Martyn wrote in his journal that his "great business" in life was the sanctification of his own soul, and he was right. The apostle Paul told Timothy to exercise himself to godliness (1 Tim. 4:7) and to preach "the doctrine which accords with godliness" (6:3). The word translated *perfect* in Matthew 5:48 means "to be complete, to be mature in character." A pediatrician examines a baby three months old and says, "This child is perfect." Of course, the child is not perfect because it can do nothing but eat, sleep, and make work for people—but for the time the child has been in the world, it is at the right stage of development. Christians can be the victims of arrested development if they ignore the Bible, prayer, worship, and service (Heb. 5:12–6:1). "Be holy, for I am holy" is repeated several times in Scripture (Lev. 11:44–45; 19:2; 20:7; 1 Pet. 1:15–16). Our goal in life is godliness, the key to every other blessing.

The model for godliness is Jesus Christ. "And Jesus increased in wisdom and stature, and in favor with God and men" (Luke 2:52). "But grow in the grace and knowledge of our Lord and Savior Jesus Christ" (2 Pet. 3:18). Jesus wants his disciples to be the mature "sons" of the Father and not struggling dependent little children (Gal. 4:4–7). Parents rejoice when their children are old enough to feed themselves and care for their own personal needs, and are able to accept responsibilities. When we were born again into God's family, God began a good work in us to prepare us for life and service, and he continues that work and brings us closer to spiritual maturity as we obey him (Phil. 1:6; Eph. 2:10). God desires that we "stand perfect and complete in all the will of God" (Col. 4:12). We must not imitate other Christians unless they are imitating Christ (1 Cor. 11:1).

The motive for following Christ is love. Christian love means that we treat others as our Father in heaven treats us, not as our enemies treat us. When our enemies abuse us, they only hurt themselves, and as we return love for hatred, we grow in the Lord as he turns curses into blessings (Deut. 23:5). Love fulfills but hatred destroys. Our love for Christ enables us to experience his love for us and then share that love with others, especially the most undeserving. The way we treat others doesn't depend on the way they treat us but on the way God treats us and them. He sends them sunshine and rain, so we should not send them storms. If we are to become perfect, complete and mature in Christ, we must suffer as he suffered and do it to the glory of God. We may not like the people who abuse us, but with the Spirit's help we can love them. Romans 12:17–21 is the mandate we follow, and if we obey, we will grow in Christian character and conduct and become more like the Master.

Do not be overcome by evil, but overcome evil with good.

Romans 12:21

6

Therefore, when you do a charitable deed, *do not sound a trumpet* before you as the hypocrites do in the synagogue and in the streets, that they may have glory from men. Assuredly, I say to you, they have their reward.

MATTHEW 6:2

A friend gifted in public relations told me, "Remember, almost everybody you meet has an invisible sign around his or her neck that reads MAKE ME FEEL IMPORTANT." Paying attention to people in Christian love is a proper thing to do, so long as our motives are pure, but catering to people just to get praise and recognition for ourselves is out of the question. That approach was especially true of the scribes and Pharisees in the first century. Giving to the poor, praying, and fasting were basic religious practices for the Jewish people, and Jesus exhorted the people not to "blow their own horns" when they were observing them. Everybody appreciates being appreciated, but to fish for compliments or to call attention to our achievements is not the Christian approach to life. There are three sources of praise, but Jesus endorsed only one of them and that's the one we should practice.

We can arouse praise from others. The scribes and Pharisees honored and praised each other but forgot about striving to receive the praise that comes only from the Lord (John 5:44; 12:43). In short, they were more concerned about reputation than character. It's not likely that Jesus was speaking about actual trumpets, for no Jew would blow a trumpet in the synagogue. Rather, he was illustrating the impropriety of calling attention to our achievements just so others can praise us. When people feel pressured to praise others, their praise is bound to be insincere. If human praise is your goal, then you can receive your reward—*but that is the end of the rewards*. You cannot receive your reward twice. Receive it from people and you won't receive it from God.

We can manufacture praise for ourselves. I am warned not to let my left hand know what my right hand is doing (Matt. 6:3). Why? Because I would immediately start *patting myself on the back.* "For whoever exalts himself will be humbled, and he who humbles himself will be exalted" (Luke 14:11). The Bible records the tragedies of numerous people whose pride inflated their egos. David was humble and became king while King Saul was proud and lost his crown. "Is not this great Babylon, that I have built for a royal dwelling by my mighty power and for the honor of my majesty?" King Nebuchadnezzar spoke those words (Dan. 4:30) and lived like a beast for the next seven years. Moses's pride when he smote the rock at Kadesh cost him the privilege of entering the Promised Land (Num. 20:1–13), and Peter's pride in boasting of his loyalty to Jesus resulted in his three humiliating denials (John 13:36–38). The rich farmer who boasted of his success died that very night (Luke 12:13–21), and the Pharisee whose temple prayer was only an egotistical press release went home in worse condition than when he came (18:9–14).

We can receive praise from God alone. The important thing is that our motives are pure, for the Lord sees our hearts. Giving is right. God commands it; people have needs and we ought to help meet those needs. But we give not because we want a reward but because it glorifies God, meets needs, and builds Christian character. God doesn't have to reward us, for we owe him our obedience; but in his grace he chooses to reward us. One day in heaven we will lay our rewards at the feet of Jesus (Rev. 4:10), for everything good comes from the generous heart of God. Hallelujah!

> For all things come from You,
> And of Your own we have given You.
> 1 Chronicles 29:14

7

> Now if God so clothes the grass of the field, which today is, and tomorrow is thrown into the oven, will He not much more clothe you, *O you of little faith?*

MATTHEW 6:30

Everybody has faith in someone or something, no matter how much they may deny it. If you endorse a check or even deposit money in the bank, you have faith. If you give a prescription to a pharmacist and later take the medicine, you are exercising faith. To drive on the highway or even to step into an elevator and push a button requires faith. The most important factor is the *object* of our faith, which for the Christian is Almighty God. Christian faith is living with confidence that God will keep his promises, and this leads us to obedience and endurance, no matter what the circumstances and consequences might be. We walk and work and war by faith.

Every true believer has some measure of faith (Rom. 12:3), and that measure can increase as we walk with the Lord, even to the level of "great faith" (Matt. 8:10; 15:28). In our text, Jesus rebukes his disciples for their "little faith," a phrase he often used. If you examine those texts, you will learn some of the characteristics of "little-faith" believers.

Little-faith people are *prone to worry*, which is the message of our text. If our faith does not operate in the affairs of daily life, it will never operate in the great challenges of ministry or spiritual warfare. Faith in God is the secret of a worry-free heart (6:25–34). Everything must be brought to the Lord in prayer if we expect to enjoy his peace (Phil. 4:6–7). The early church emphasized prayer and the ministry of the Word (Acts 6:4), and both demand faith and help to build faith.

Little-faith people are *easily frightened*. A sudden storm broke out on the Sea of Galilee and the disciples were terribly frightened, *but Jesus was asleep*! (Matt. 8:23–27) The men woke the Lord and cried, "Save us! We are perishing!" Jesus stilled the storm on the sea *but he could not still the fear in their hearts*. Their problem was their little faith, and that may be your problem. Charles Spurgeon said, "Little faith will take your soul to heaven, but great faith will bring heaven to your soul."

Little-faith people are *indecisive*. According to Matthew 14:22–33, Jesus deliberately sent his disciples into a storm one night on the Sea of Galilee, while he remained behind. In the middle of the night, he came to them *walking on the water*. "Lord, if it is You," cried Peter, "command me to come to You on the water" (v. 28). Jesus said one word: "Come!" *And Peter walked on the water to meet Jesus*. But then Peter took his eyes off Jesus and began to look at the huge waves and to feel the strong wind. What happened? He began to sink! "Lord, save me!" he cried, and Jesus rescued him (vv. 30–31). Remember, Peter knew that body of water like you know your backyard, yet he became afraid and "halted between two opinions." Beware of being "double-minded" (James 1:8), but this is the plight of the little-faith person.

Jesus compared faith to a mustard seed, one of the smallest seeds known (Matt. 17:20). But the size of the seed is immaterial; it's the life within the seed that counts. Plant the seed and eventually you will have a large plant (13:31–32). Faith is like that tiny seed: if the seed is planted in the heart and nurtured, it will produce the plant. The Bible is "the words of faith" (1 Tim. 4:6), and the more we feed on God's truth, the stronger our faith will become. As we claim God's promises in prayer, our faith will mature.

According to your faith let it be done to you.

Matthew 9:29 TNIV

8

> *Enter by the narrow gate*; for wide is the gate and broad is the way that leads to destruction, and there are many who go in by it. Because narrow is the gate and difficult is the way which leads to life, and there are few who find it.
>
> MATTHEW 7:13–14

After a night of prayer, our Lord chose his twelve disciples and then preached their ordination sermon, which we call the Sermon on the Mount. In it he explained true righteousness and exposed the artificial righteousness of the scribes and Pharisees (Matt. 5:20). Churches today have counterfeit Christians in their midst, so this sermon applies to us. The metaphor of the gates and roads helps us examine ourselves to see if we truly know the Lord.

The privilege of choice. We are made in the image of God, and the Lord does not "assault" us to make us obey him. In his Word, he explains the basic truths we need to know and urges us to make the right decision. If we reject the will of God, we suffer for it. Some people don't like to make decisions and drift from one problem to another, or else let others decide for them. But life's decisions come at us like bullets and it's dangerous to delay. People may pray for us and counsel us, but we must make the decisions. There is no place for neutrality or compromise. We either abandon our worldly luggage and go through the narrow gate onto the narrow road, or we hold on to everything and walk through the broad gate onto the broad road. We make the decisions and we experience the consequences.

The peril of illusion. Going through the narrow gate ("strait" as in straitjacket) and walking on the narrow way means we must leave behind everything that is not consistent

20

with a dedicated Christian life. Jesus described it as "taking up your cross," and we can't carry our cross and our worldly baggage at the same time. But beware of the illusions in the world. It appears that the broad gate is the easier entrance, but that is pure illusion. "Strive to enter through the narrow gate," says Jesus in Luke 13:24; and the word translated "strive" gives us the English word *agonize*. It pictures an athlete giving his or her very best and paying a price to win the race. *From start to finish, the Christian life is not an easy life.* "We must through many tribulations enter the kingdom of God" (Acts 14:22). The broad, crowded road seems to be the easier way to go, but that road leads to destruction. The world's illusions will only lead you astray. Beware!

The promise of life. The choice we make is a matter of life or death. "I have come that they may have life," said Jesus, "and that they may have it more abundantly" (John 10:10). The way is difficult, but it's the only way to eternal life. The pleasures of sin do not last (Heb. 11:25), but the joys of eternal life do not end. What a tragedy to come to the end of life and discover that we have not lived!

"There is a way that seems right to a man, but its end is the way of death." That statement is found in both Proverbs 14:12 and 16:25, so it must be important. God sets before us two ways, the difficult way of life and the easy way of sin and destruction. God's counsel to us is to "Choose life" (Deut. 30:19).

> You will show me the path of life;
> In Your presence is fullness of joy;
> At Your right hand are pleasures forevermore.
>
> Psalm 16:11

9

Ask, and it will be given to you; *seek, and you will find*; knock, and it will be opened to you.

MATTHEW 7:7

Unless we as God's people learn to pray as we should, we will never move toward spiritual maturity or have effective ministries that will glorify God. "However, brethren, whether we like it or not, remember, *asking is the rule of the kingdom*." Those words are as true today as when Charles Haddon Spurgeon spoke them on Sunday morning, October 1, 1882, at the Metropolitan Tabernacle in London. "You do not have because you do not ask" (James 4:2).

But prayer is much more than asking and receiving, although that is essential; prayer is also *seeking and finding*. Prayer is not simply a conversation with God in which we tell him all our needs. *Prayer is also a journey with God during which he shows us himself and his resources.* Jesus said, "Take My yoke upon you and learn from Me" (Matt. 11:29). Learn what? The greatness of his character and the immeasurable vastness of his wealth. If our fellowship with God in prayer consists only of "give me this and give me that," we are to be pitied. We need to pray with Moses, "Please, show me Your glory" (Exod. 33:18), and with David, "Your face, LORD, I will seek" (Ps. 27:8). When we pray the familiar Lord's Prayer, our first requests (before we say "give us") focus on glorifying God's name, hastening the coming of God's kingdom, and doing God's will. Those are priorities.

The first question Jesus asked his disciples was, "What do you seek?" (John 1:38), and he asks that question of us today. If we don't know what we are seeking, our journey will be a waste of time. "And do you seek great things for yourself? Do not seek them" (Jer. 45:5). To be sure, "things"

22

are important and God knows that we need them (Matt. 6:32); but we must remember our spiritual priorities. "But seek first the kingdom of God and His righteousness, and all these things shall be added to you" (v. 33). "Things" are fringe benefits, but God's rule and God's righteousness are essentials. God is "a rewarder of those who diligently seek Him" (Heb. 11:6). Just as parents love to spend time with their children and share love and understanding, so our Father is pleased when we get alone with him, ponder his Word, worship him, and open our hearts in full surrender.

Have you ever journeyed in prayer through the Beatitudes (Matt. 5:1–12)? What a journey that is! These profound statements are like mirrors that help us examine ourselves, and then they become windows that reveal the greatness of the character of God. *As we behold the beauty of Jesus, God's glory shines and we become more like him* (2 Cor. 3:18)! When you finish journeying in the Beatitudes, journey through a psalm, such as Psalm 15 or 19. What does God say to us about himself, about ourselves, about the grace he has for each need and challenge? One of the richest journeys is through the prison prayers of the apostle Paul (Eph. 1:15–23; 3:14–21; Phil. 1:3–11; Col. 1:9–12).

Our Lord added "knock, and it will be opened to you," and the little word *it* refers to a door of service being opened by the Lord; for in Scripture, an "open door" speaks of ministry. "For a great and effective door has opened to me," wrote Paul (1 Cor. 16:9; *see* Col. 4:3; Rev. 3:8). God blesses us that we might be a blessing to others. What we keep, we may lose, but what we give, we keep forever. When we ask, we get; when we seek, we grow; and when we knock, we give. This is a balanced Christian life.

See, I have set before you an open door, and no one can shut it.

Revelation 3:8

10

The centurion answered and said, *"Lord, I am not worthy* that You should come under my roof. But only speak a word, and my servant will be healed."

MATTHEW 8:8

When he was not traveling in ministry, Jesus made his "headquarters" in Capernaum, the city of Peter, Andrew, James, and John. It was the principal harbor for the many fishermen on the Sea of Galilee and was surrounded by farmland that was especially fruitful. Capernaum was located on a major trade route, so it was not a simple village but a bustling cosmopolitan city, which explains why Rome had stationed soldiers there. In the four Gospels and the Book of Acts, you meet seven centurions, all of whom are presented as honorable men who treated Jesus and the Christians with dignity and kindness. Three questions come to mind from this account of Jesus and the centurion.

How do our friends see us? This centurion had been especially kind to the Jews in Capernaum and had built a synagogue for them. When the elders of the synagogue brought the centurion's request to Jesus that he come and heal the servant, they argued the centurion's case by saying he had built them a synagogue and therefore was worthy of receiving his help (Luke 7:3–5). But the centurion openly stated, "I am not worthy!" The Jewish elders knew that, according to their tradition, a Jew was defiled if he entered a Gentile's house, although this would not have prevented Jesus from helping the servant. The Gentile officer knew more about Jesus than the elders did, because he said, "I also am a man under authority" (Matt. 8:9). Note that word *also*. He believed Jesus acted under God's authority, a remarkable conviction for a Roman soldier.

24

How do we see ourselves? The centurion did not exalt himself. He admitted he was under authority to his superior officers and ultimately to the emperor, but this authority gave him no power to heal his beloved dying servant. Surely the centurion knew about our Lord's miraculous healings in other places. A Roman officer could issue all sorts of commands in a conquered land, but this man was not abusive. Like Cornelius in Acts 10, he used his authority to help others and not to display his own "greatness." Wherever there are humble hearts, God can do his work and bring them truth and life (Isa. 57:15). "When pride comes, then comes shame; but with the humble is wisdom" (Prov. 11:2). The centurion's humility brought him a great commendation from Jesus!

How does Jesus see us? Jesus must have known about the centurion's love for his servant, and the man's statement about authority revealed his faith in the power of Jesus's words. But Jesus said nothing about the synagogue or the generosity of the centurion. Rather, he was greatly impressed with the soldier's faith in the power of the words Jesus spoke. Could the soldier have learned this from a report of the healing of the nobleman's son in Capernaum (John 4:46–54), when Jesus healed the boy *from a distance?* The centurion was saying, "Just say the word and my servant will be healed." God created the universe simply by speaking the word. "For He spoke, and it was done; He commanded, and it stood fast" (Ps. 33:9). Jesus marveled at the man's faith, a man who was a pagan Gentile! He also marveled at a Gentile woman's faith (Matt. 15:28) and at *the unbelief of the Jews* (Mark 6:1–6).

The Lord is planning to work through us in the lives of people and places we know nothing about today; but if we walk in his will, we shall share in the blessing. Are we under his authority and trusting him? If so, get ready for a miracle!

He sent His word and healed them.

Psalm 107:20

11

When He saw the multitudes, *He was moved with compassion* for them, because they were weary and scattered, like sheep having no shepherd.

MATTHEW 9:36

Our eyes usually see the things that interest our hearts. Children see candy stores and toy shops, while their parents see "sale" signs. I notice used book stores and my wife finds fabric shops. When Jesus saw the multitudes, he had a concern for the people he came to save.

Compassion. Our English word comes from two Latin words that together mean "to suffer with another, to endure pain with another." The Greek word in our text is more dramatic because it refers to the inner viscera of the human body being greatly moved. A person with compassion is stirred to the very depths and feels pain because others are suffering. Three times Matthew tells us that Jesus had compassion on the multitudes (9:36; 14:14; 15:32), and his heart also went out to needy individuals—two blind men (Matt. 20:34), a leper (Mark 1:41), a demoniac (5:19), a sorrowing widow (Luke 7:13), and a demonized boy (Mark 9:22). In three of his parables, Jesus spoke of compassion (Matt. 18:27; Luke 10:33; 15:20). In our text (Matt. 9:36–37), he saw the multitudes as helpless, wandering sheep being abused by their shepherds. He also saw the crowds as fields of grain, ready for the harvest. The sheep would wander away and be killed by predators, and the harvest would go to waste, all for the lack of people with compassion. Does that fact move us?

Intercession. Our Lord's remedy for this heartbreaking situation was *prayer* (v. 38), asking God to send compassionate laborers to care for the flocks and fields. *When was the last time we asked God to send out laborers? Have we asked him*

26

to call them from our own family? The doctor told my mother she would never raise me past the age of two because I had a problem with my blood, but his prediction was never fulfilled. Why? Because I had a godly great-grandfather who prayed there would be a preacher of the gospel in every generation of our family, *and there has been.* I pray daily that the Lord will send laborers into his harvest field, and I always add, "And call some from our family"—and he has. Compassion and intercession must go together.

Dedication. When we start praying for God to send laborers, we must remember that he often starts to answer *in and through the intercessor* (Eph. 3:20). I'm sure Moses prayed for God to deliver his people from slavery in Egypt, and God called him to be that deliverer. Nehemiah wept and prayed over the sad state of Jerusalem, and the Lord sent him as governor to rebuild the walls (Neh. 1–2). It was in a prayer meeting that the Lord called Paul and Barnabas to take the gospel to the Gentiles (Acts 13:1–3). Therefore, when we pray, we must first give ourselves to the Lord; otherwise, we might only be praying from the lips and not the heart. If I am not willing to serve in his will, what right do I have to ask others to serve?

Our great High Priest has compassion and concern for us (Heb. 4:15–16), and we ought to have compassion for others. Let's start at home with our own family and neighbors, then we can intercede for our church family and saints and sinners all over the world. The word meaning "compassion" is found in one form or another in Ephesians 4:32 ("tenderhearted"), Philippians 2:1 ("affection"), Colossians 3:12 ("tender mercies"), and 1 Peter 3:8 ("tenderhearted"), and they all add up to *compassion.* We are never more like Jesus than when we are compassionate.

> O Lord, I pray, please let Your ear be attentive to the prayer of Your servant, and to the prayer of Your servants who desire to fear Your name.
>
> Nehemiah 1:11

12

> Come to me, all you who labor and are heavy laden, and *I will give you rest*. Take My yoke upon you and learn from Me, for I am gentle and lowly in heart, and you will find rest for your souls. For My yoke is easy and My burden is light.

MATTHEW 11:28–30

Historians have a challenging time thinking up names for the various eras in human history. We have had the "Aspirin Age," the "Dark Ages," the "Middle Ages," and the "Age of Enlightenment," to name but a few; but I think the best name for the period from the Second World War to the present would be the "Restless Age." To me it appears to be a time when restless people have been using sedatives, psychiatric help, and other devices to escape the problems and pressures of daily life. You can go to the drugstore and purchase sleep but you can't buy rest, and the entertainment you buy is only a temporary distraction that often leaves you more restless than when you started. The only offer of rest that is valid is the one Jesus gives us in our text. He invites us to take three simple steps of faith.

Take Jesus as your Savior and receive rest. His simple invitation is *come*—not *go*, *work*, *buy*, or *try*—and when we come in faith, he gives us rest. This rest is a gift, but it cost him his life when he died for us on the cross. The Bible calls this rest "peace with God" (Rom. 5:1), which means that all our sins are forgiven, past, present, and future (Col. 2:13), and will never be held against us. In Greek literature, the phrase "heavy laden" in our text referred to a ship's cargo, which is a good description of the burdens people try to carry today. What wonderful security we have with Jesus as our Savior!

Surrender to Jesus your Master and find rest. "Take My yoke upon you" may sound like exchanging one burden for another, except for one thing: Jesus assures us that his yoke is easy and his burden is light. The word *easy* means "fitted, comfortable." Receiving Jesus as Savior gives us security, but yielding to him as Master gives us responsibility. This is "the peace of God" (Phil. 4:6–7). Because we are yoked to Jesus, he helps us carry the burden. Everybody you meet is wearing some kind of yoke, some responsibility that burdens them, and most of them are trying to do it alone. Those who know Jesus as Master know that he is the burden-bearer, not carrying the burdens *instead of* us but carrying them *with* us. Having God's rest doesn't mean we retire from life; no, we find rest in life, the kind of daily renewal that keeps us going in spite of the cares of life and service. He is a gracious and loving Master who knows how to plan each day so our tasks will build us, bless others, and glorify God.

Make Jesus your Friend and find deeper rest in his love. We move now from security and responsibility to *intimacy*. "You are My friends if you do whatever I command you," said Jesus. "No longer do I call you servants, for a servant does not know what his master is doing; but I have called you friends, for all things that I have heard from My Father I have made known to you" (John 15:14–15). "He made known His ways to Moses, His acts to the children of Israel" (Ps. 103:7). The nation knew *what* God was doing, but Moses knew *why* he was doing it. When we are intimate with Jesus in his Word, we grow in our knowledge of God and his will for us. We cannot control the world around us, but with God's help, we can control the world within us and experience the "peace of God, which surpasses all understanding" (Phil. 4:7). Savior + Master + Friend = rest.

> Therefore, having been justified by faith, we have peace with God through our Lord Jesus Christ.
>
> Romans 5:1

13

He said to them, "*An enemy has done this.*"

MATTHEW 13:28

e aware! As Christians, we live on a battleground, not a playground, because we have an enemy who is out to defeat us and destroy the work of the Lord. Caricatures of Satan show up in comic strips and cartoons, but he is definitely not a scarlet-horned creature with a pointed tail and a pitchfork. Ponder some of his names and titles and you will have to take the devil seriously. He is Abaddon and Apollyon, the destroyer (Rev. 9:11), the accuser (12:10), the adversary (1 Pet. 5:8), the god of this age (2 Cor. 4:4), the liar and murderer (John 8:44), and the prince of this world (14:30), to cite but a few of his titles. Jesus met Satan in the wilderness and soundly defeated him there (Matt. 4:1–11), but our Lord's definitive victory over him was at the cross (Col. 2:13–15). Every Christian shares in both of these victories if they will follow Christ's example and claim his victory by faith.

Be alert! Satan is a counterfeiter. Jesus is the Lord of the harvest who plants his people wherever he wants them to bear fruit. Because we are seeds, we have his life within us and he wants us to be fruitful and multiply ourselves as we witness to others. We must be willing to die to sin and the world and surrender ourselves completely to Christ. But wherever Jesus plants a true believer, the devil comes and plants a counterfeit. Just as there are children of God, so there are children of the devil (Matt. 3:7; John 8:44), false Christians who are religious but have never been born again (2 Cor. 11:26; 1 John 3:10–15). Satan has false ministers (2 Cor. 11:13–15) who preach a false gospel (Gal. 1:6–9) that produces a false righteousness (Rom. 10:1–4). He even has a false church (Rev. 2:9; 3:9). God's people must be alert to detect these counterfeits and make sure they don't creep into places of leadership in the church (2 Pet. 2:1). We must stay alert, for it was while the workers slept that the devil planted his counterfeits in the field. To us this means not physical sleep but spiritual lethargy, a careless and casual attitude toward the Christian life.

Be available! Jesus wants to plant us where we will bear fruit for his glory. In the parable of the sower, the soil represents different kinds of hearts, but in this parable, "the field is the world" (Matt. 13:38). Jesus is both the sower and the owner of the field, and he plants his people where he wants them to bear fruit. "Most assuredly, I say to you," said Jesus, "unless a grain of wheat falls into the ground and dies, it remains alone; but if it dies, it produces much fruit" (John 12:24). The Lord may have planted you in a school, an office, a military camp, a hospital, a store, a quiet home, or a noisy neighborhood, but no matter where he has planted you, be sure you are "rooted and built up in Him" (Col. 2:7) and "rooted and grounded in love" (Eph. 3:17). A friend of mine, now in heaven, had to be in the hospital for several weeks, and during that time led several nurses to faith in Christ. Bloom wherever you are planted!

Be assured! The servants in the parable wanted to weed out the foreign plants, but the master told them not to lest they damage the crop. We must be careful not to get detoured into other activities and rob our Master of the harvest he deserves. We are living in a society that has in it the true and the false, and only Jesus can help us so to live that people will recognize the reality of our testimony and want to trust the Savior. Take the "long view" of witnessing. The farmer patiently waits for the seed to germinate and ultimately bear fruit. We can be assured that in due season we shall have a harvest if we do not get discouraged or detoured.

> Do not be deceived, God is not mocked; for whatever a man sows, that he will also reap.
>
> Galatians 6:7

14

He departed from there by boat to *a deserted place by Himself*. But when the multitudes heard it, they followed Him on foot from the cities.

MATTHEW 14:13

From the beginning of our Lord's public ministry, great crowds of people followed him, and there were times when he had to get away from the crowd. I have identified at least eight occasions on which Jesus left the crowds and went off alone or with his disciples: After his baptism (Matt. 3:13–4:11), After a busy day of ministry (Mark 1:32–35), After healing a leper (Mark 1:40–45), After the death of John the Baptist (Matt. 14:1–13), After feeding the five thousand (John 6:1–15), Before calling the twelve apostles (Luke 6:12–16), After the apostles' report on their ministry (Mark 6:30–32), Before his suffering and death (Matt. 26:36–45).

Our Lord's baptism was the signal that his ministry had begun. The Father spoke words of approval and encouragement and the Spirit endowed him with power. But then the Spirit drove Jesus into the wilderness where he fasted for forty days and encountered and defeated the devil. Our high and holy hours of spiritual enrichment must be balanced with dark days of sacrifice and conflict. After a busy evening of healing in Capernaum, Jesus had a short night of sleep and then arose very early to pray and prepare for another busy day. We must begin each day spending time alone with God (Isa. 40:31; 50:4–7).

Jesus healed a leper and told him not to tell others, but the man told everybody about Jesus. (Jesus instructs us to tell everybody and we say nothing!) Jesus had to go to a deserted place, but the crowds found him anyway. Jesus was a servant, not a celebrity; he knew the motives in the hearts of the people mobbing him. When we feel successful, it's time to get alone with God.

The death of John the Baptist must have moved Jesus deeply, and he went away alone to mourn. After all, his own death was also on the schedule. God's people are human and need to work their way through sorrow and pain. Jesus prayed alone all night before choosing his twelve apostles (Luke 6:12–16), and at crisis experiences in our lives we need to spend extra time seeking the Father's will. When the apostles returned to report on their itinerant ministry, Jesus took them to a deserted place so they could rest and be spiritually refreshed. Vance Havner used to remind us, "If we don't come apart and rest, we will just come apart." There are times when taking a day off or a vacation, or even a brief nap, might be the most spiritual thing we can do.

Our Lord's experience in Gethsemane before his arrest prepared him for the agonies of the trials—the mockery, the whippings, and then the crucifixion. We can never fully experience the suffering he endured, but we can follow the example of his surrender in the garden. Jesus took the cup of sacrifice and drank it, saying, "Not my will but your will be done." Every dedicated child of God has Gethsemane experiences and can find victory in prayer and submission.

In the difficult challenges of the Christian life, we must not try to escape, as did David (Ps. 55:6) and Jeremiah (Jer. 9:2). We leave the crowd that we may return to the crowd with new strength for ministry. The most important part of the Christian life is the part that only God sees: our times alone with him.

> But those who wait on the LORD
> Shall renew their strength;
> They shall mount up with wings like eagles,
> They shall run and not be weary,
> They shall walk and not faint.
>
> Isaiah 40:31

15

He said, *"Bring them here to Me."*

The word "them" in our text refers to the five loaves and two fish in the hands of the lad that Andrew found in that huge crowd. (Andrew was gifted at connecting people with Jesus. *See* John 1:40–42; 12:20–26.) But how could the disciples feed over five thousand people with such a small supply of food? Even Andrew asked, "But what are they among so many?" (John 6:9). They didn't have sufficient funds in the treasury to purchase food, so the disciples had concluded that the best solution to the problem was to send everybody away. But our Lord's compassion for people put an end to that suggestion. In my own Christian life and ministry, when the resources were very low and the demands very high, the Lord has frequently said to me, "You give them something to eat" (Matt. 14:16). But Jesus always "knew what He would do" (John 6:6) and the resources were always provided. What must we do to receive his provision?

Be sure your heart is right. The heart of every problem is the problem in the heart. Jesus had compassion for the hungry crowd and refused to dismiss them. I used to tell my ministerial students that the easiest way to solve church problems is to get rid of all the people. It's easy to care for an empty building! But true ministry involves people, and we must learn to love them. The Lord never allows his obedient servants to get into circumstances they cannot handle with his divine help.

Survey the resources. When Andrew found the lad with the lunch, he made the mistake of measuring the demands by the lunch instead of measuring the lunch by the Lord. The lunch was small but their God was great! No matter how

34

little we may think we have, we must remember that the Lord delights in taking the little things, the weak things, yes, and "the things which are not" (1 Cor. 1:27–28) to accomplish great things for his glory.

Give all you have to Jesus. The loaves and fish in the boy's hands were only a lunch, and in Andrew's hands only a contribution—but in the hands of Jesus they became a miracle. "Bring them here to Me" is one of the most gracious invitations anywhere in Scripture. Whatever battles you are fighting or problems or burdens you are carrying, put them into the hands of the Lord and then do what he commands. The miracle didn't occur in the hands of the disciples but in the hands of Jesus. Divine power multiplied the food and human hands distributed it.

Look up to heaven. It was a Jewish practice at meals to look up and bless God for his provision. "Give us this day our daily bread" is our request at the start of the day and we say "Thank you, Lord" as we sit at the table and eat. Obeying the command of Deuteronomy 8:10, my Swedish relatives also prayed at the end of the meal. In this simple gesture of looking up, Jesus reminded the crowd where the food was coming from. To God be the glory!

Work together in serving. There was plenty to eat and the disciples did their job well. They also filled twelve baskets full of the leftovers. (Never waste a miracle! I'm sure they gave the boy a supply to take home.) The crowd was so impressed they wanted to make Jesus king, but he went off on a mountain to pray (John 6:15).

When we find ourselves troubled about things that are beyond us, let's obey the voice of Jesus: "Bring them here to Me." We are not manufacturers; we are distributors.

When you have eaten and are full, then you shall bless the LORD your God for the good land which He has given you.

Deuteronomy 8:10

16

> And I also say to you that you are Peter, and on
> this rock I *will build My church*, and the gates of
> Hades shall not prevail against it.

MATTHEW 16:18

This is the first appearance of the word *church* in the
New Testament. From this text to Revelation 22:16,
it is found 114 times. This first reference should elicit
several responses from those of us who love Christ and his
church, both local and universal. Consider some of these
responses.

Encouragement—Christ is building. In spite of the chaos
and destruction we see in human history and in today's world,
Jesus is building his church. Satan is Apollyon, the destroyer
(Rev. 9:11), but Christ the carpenter is the builder. The word
church in the New Testament doesn't refer to a material building, formerly called "the church house." The word *church*
refers to an assembly of saved people who gather together to
worship the Lord, encourage one another, and seek to spread
the gospel around the world.

Amazement—Christ is building a church. Christ is the
foundation and cornerstone of his church (1 Cor. 3:11; Eph.
2:20) and believers are the living stones (1 Pet. 2:5). Whenever
a sinner anywhere in the world trusts Christ, a new stone
is added to the building. No matter what may happen to
civilization, the church is indestructible and will last forever. What we do to serve Jesus and his church will also last
forever, so don't despair. The church is a unique group of
people. "There is neither Jew nor Gentile, neither slave nor
free, neither male nor female, for you are all one in Christ
Jesus" (Gal. 3:28 TNIV).

Discernment—it is Christ's church. I frequently hear people say, "Now, at *my* church"—but the church is not theirs; it belongs to Christ. He purchased it with his blood (Acts 20:28). It's unfortunate that some congregations forget this and allow Diotrephes and his family to "run the church" to please themselves (3 John 9–11). More than one minister's heart has been broken to see "church bosses" take over and "run" the ministry. Every church member needs to find out his or her spiritual gift and put it to work for the glory of the Lord; let's speak the truth in love (Eph. 4:15) whenever it's necessary to criticize or make changes. Every "living stone" in the church must be in the right place or it will become a stumbling block and a source of trouble. Only the Spirit of God, using the Word of God, can give the church the leadership it needs, and he will do so if we pray and search the Scriptures daily.

Achievement—Christ will finish the work. The world, the flesh, and the devil cannot prevent our Lord from one day presenting his church "faultless before the presence of His glory with exceeding joy" (Jude 24). The church today is a "work in progress," which means it is far from perfect; but one day in heaven it will be "a glorious church, not having spot or wrinkle or any such thing" (Eph. 5:27). Spots come from defilement and wrinkles come from decay, but both will be gone forever when we see Christ. When Moses finished building the tabernacle and Solomon the temple, God moved in with great glory. But when Jesus finishes his church, *the church will move out and up to heaven to share in Christ's glory.* What a day that will be.

Christ loves his church, and so should every believer.

[His church] should be holy and without blemish.

Ephesians 5:27

17

The young man said to Him, "All these things I have kept from my youth. *What do I still lack?*"

*S*earching. Proud people don't think they lack anything and weak people think they lack everything, but people like this young man are a unique species. He thought he had everything but couldn't understand why life wasn't working out as he had planned. He had money, character, reputation, and religion, but apparently he didn't have peace in his heart. Something was missing and he didn't know what it was. Hearing Jesus teach in the temple or the marketplace may have attracted him to the Savior. Whatever his motive, he ran up to Jesus and began to ask questions. Jesus pointed him to the commandments of the Jewish law, but the young man then became evasive. "Which ones?" he asked, and Jesus quoted from the second table of the law. But the law is not a buffet from which you pick and choose the regulations you want to obey. "For whoever shall keep the whole law, and yet stumble in one point, he is guilty of all" (James 2:10). The law is a mirror that reveals our blemishes to us, but the young man saw no blemishes. He didn't seem to know that hatred was like murder in the heart and lust like adultery (Matt. 5:21–30).

Finding. Jesus gave him the solution to his problem: he was covetous and had to break the power material possessions had over him. Had the young man reviewed the second table of the law, he would have met "You shall not covet" (Exod. 20:17), and that might have convicted him and led to his conversion, for there can be no true conversion without conviction. Our Lord gave him three instructions: go and sell what you have, give it to the poor, and follow me (Matt. 19:21). "Take heed and beware of covetousness, for one's life does not consist in the abundance of the things he possesses" (Luke 12:15). Like many people today, the man had resources for the outer journey of life, but he lacked resources for the inner journey of the spirit. He had been accumulating things and starving. his spirit. He quickly took inventory of his possessions and decided it was too costly to part with them. And as for following Jesus—a poor man—he saw no future in that.

Losing. Apparently the man said nothing further to Jesus. He merely arose, turned, and walked away. He was humble and enthusiastic when he first ran up to Jesus, but now he was sorrowful and disappointed. By rejecting the will of God, the man lost both his wealth and a new life in Christ. Had he surrendered to the Lord, he would have experienced forgiveness and a joyful and exciting new life in the Lord. But his wrong decision sent him back home to the same old routine with plenty of money to support it. Jesus shocked his disciples when he said, "It is hard for a rich man to enter the kingdom of heaven" (Matt. 19:23), for the Jews thought that riches were a mark of the favor of God. The young ruler kept his wealth but forfeited Jesus. He was still a ruler but he lost the privilege of being a disciple of the King. He would continue his outward journey and become richer and more influential, but his inward journey was halted.

"Who then can be saved?" asked the disciples. Jesus made it clear that we cannot save ourselves, either with money or good works, nor can we save others. Salvation is of the Lord; only he can do the impossible—and it cost Jesus his life for this salvation to be available. As the children of God, in Jesus Christ we have everything—and lack nothing.

> His divine power has given us everything we need for a godly life through our knowledge of him who called us by his own glory and goodness.
>
> 2 Peter 1:3 TNIV

18

Then Peter answered and said to Him, "See, we have left all and followed You. *Therefore what shall we have?*"

MATTHEW 19:27

Peter's question sounds very selfish, but not when you consider the context. Note that he says "we," for he spoke for the other eleven disciples as well. All twelve were perplexed. The rich young ruler had just walked away, unhappy and disappointed, refusing to part with his wealth. But the disciples had given up everything to follow Jesus. If a rich man had a hard time entering the kingdom of God, what hope was there for these poor disciples? Jesus assured them that their sacrifices would be rewarded, for they would be blessed in their present life and amply rewarded in the future (Matt. 19:28–30). "Blessed are the poor in spirit, for theirs is the kingdom of heaven" (5:3). But this entire event (including the parable that follows) gives us some important instructions about serving the Lord.

Be careful not to focus on yourself. The world's attitude toward service is, "What will *I* get out of it?" The parable of the workers (20:1–16) describes the early morning workers as demanding a contract, while those hired later accepted the owner's promise of, "Whatever is right, I will give you" (vv. 2–4). It's dangerous to negotiate the will of God, because the Lord will always give us far more than we have earned or than we deserve. We are only robbing ourselves when we question God's generosity and insist that he give us just what we want. "If you then, being evil, know how to give good gifts to your children, how much more will your Father who is in heaven give good things to those who ask Him?" (7:11). If our concern is to reward ourselves, we are playing right into the hands of Satan, who promised our first parents, "You shall be as God." Satan always has a "special deal," but the dividends are deadly. God is generous; trust him.

Avoid focusing on other people. The early morning employees in the parable watched to see how much the other workers were paid, and they jumped to the conclusion that they would receive more than they had bargained for. They were wrong. *They got what they bargained for!* You and I have enough to do handling our own lives without meddling with the lives of others. Peter made this same mistake after the Easter breakfast with Jesus (John 21). Jesus dealt with Peter's sins and then said, "Follow me." This was his recommissioning as an apostle. John also got up and began to follow, and Peter turned around and saw him. "But Lord, what about this man?" Peter asked, and Jesus replied, "If I wish that he remain till I come, what is that to you? You follow Me" (vv. 20–22). Watching other believers can lead to envy or pride, both of which are abominable sins. Paul makes it clear that each believer will receive his or her own reward when we stand at the judgment seat of Christ (1 Cor. 3:8).

Focus your heart and mind on Jesus and do his will. When we received Jesus, we received everything we need for living the Christian life. God did not spare his only Son, so we can trust him to give us everything else. No matter what sacrifices we make, they are nothing compared to the sacrifices Jesus made for us. We don't live on explanations or contracts; we live on the promises of God. God has blessed his children "with every spiritual blessing in the heavenly places in Christ" (Eph. 1:3), and his promise is, "Ask, and it will be given to you" (Matt. 7:7). Peter moved from "What will we get?" to "What I do have I give you" (Acts 3:6), and brought glory to the name of the Lord.

> He who did not spare His own Son, but delivered Him up for us all, how shall He not with Him also freely give us all things?
>
> Romans 8:32

19

And I was afraid, and went and hid your talent in the ground. Look, there *you have what is yours*.

MATTHEW 25:25

The Lord doesn't want to receive things from us exactly as they were when he gave them to us. He wants us to use our God-given ability to accomplish his will and expand the kingdom. Just as earthly parents are happy when their children achieve, so our heavenly Father wants to have the joy of "promoting" us and rewarding us for our faithfulness in doing his will.

We are born with abilities. Some people have many abilities while others have very few. The American Declaration of Independence tells us "all men are created equal," but this means equal in the sight of God and the law, not in the sight of one another. When people are born again, the Spirit gives them gifts to match their abilities. The Master knows us intimately and always knows where we can serve best. He expects us to have faith that he will help us do the job well.

We are given opportunities to match our abilities and gifts. The talents in the parable represent opportunities to use our abilities. As we are faithful to serve, we grow in faith and works and the Lord is able to give us more work to do. David started as a servant of King Saul, soothing the king with his harp music. Then he became a soldier and a commander of soldiers, winning many difficult battles. Eventually he was made king and led his armies to great victories. If we are faithful, we will move from a few things to many things and from being servants to being rulers. Each new assignment gives us opportunity to grow. The one-talent man thought he was not important and ended up rebuked and unrewarded *because he did nothing*. He despised his one ability and opportunity, he feared his master instead of obeying him, and he wasted his opportunity to please the master and grow in ministry.

We must accept our responsibilities. Many people in Scripture hesitated to accept the plans God had for their lives—Moses, Gideon, and Jeremiah, for example—but the Lord saw them through. *It is a sin to do nothing.* Note in Matthew 25:41–46 that the "goats" were condemned because they did not minister to those in need. There are sins of omission as well as sins of commission. The servant should have been thankful for his one talent, appreciative of his generous master and happy to go to work investing his talent and watching it grow. The master was gone "a long time," so there was plenty of opportunity to accomplish something. Instead of making progress he made excuses, and people who are good at excuses are rarely good at anything else. "The lazy man is wiser in his own eyes than seven men who can answer sensibly" (Prov. 26:16). Someone has said that "responsibility is our response to God's ability," and our first response must be, "Yes, Lord, I will obey."

We will face accountability. It's a serious matter to serve the Lord, and with responsibility comes accountability. "For we shall all stand before the judgment seat of Christ" (Rom. 14:10). The issue will not be how much ability we had but whether we were faithful to use our abilities and opportunities to please our Master. "Moreover it is required in stewards that one be found faithful" (1 Cor. 4:2). We are not all successful in the same way, but we can all be faithful in our work and bring glory to God. Jesus is a loving Master who knows just what we can do and how much we can bear, so we need never fear his will. Winston Churchill said, "We make a living by what we get; we make a life by what we give." Let's give our best to Jesus and really live!

> For everyone to whom much is given, from him much will be required; and to whom much has been committed, of him they will ask the more.
>
> Luke 12:48

20

And the King will answer and say to them, "Assuredly, I say to you, inasmuch as you did it to one of the least of these My brethren, *you did it to Me.*"

MATTHEW 25:40

Whether we meet a Christian or an unbeliever, we must keep Jesus in the picture, for a believer is someone in whom Jesus lives, and an unbeliever is someone for whom Jesus died. If Jesus is in the picture, we will treat each person as we would treat Christ himself. If this truth doesn't improve our "people skills," nothing will.

There is joy in doing something for others and doing it as though we were doing it for our Master. There is also a reward in store for us if we follow this pattern. One day, Jesus will reward those who have served faithfully and sacrificed for others *for the sake of Jesus Christ*. It isn't a question of whether or not these people deserved this kind treatment, because if the Lord gave *us* what we deserved, we would be condemned forever! It's simply a question of pleasing Jesus and doing what he would do if he were still serving on earth.

But along with the joyful blessing of doing good things for others, there is also the danger of losing the blessing by doing nothing. There are sins of omission as well as sins of commission. "Therefore, to one who knows the right thing to do and does not do it, to him it is sin" (James 4:17 NASB). The familiar parable of the Good Samaritan illustrates this vividly (Luke 10:25–37). The thieves were guilty of sins of commission, for they robbed the man, beat him, and left him to die. The priest and the Levite were guilty of sins of omission, for they passed by the victim and did nothing. No doubt both of them had excuses that quieted their consciences. The priest might have thought, *Those thieves might still be in the area, so I had better hurry on. Anyway, I have sacred duties to perform at the temple. The Levite is coming behind me. No doubt he'll help this poor man.* The Levite could have said to himself, *The priest didn't do anything, so why should I?* Each of us is either somebody's excuse for doing nothing or somebody's encouragement for doing right.

As God's people, we must first give ourselves to the Lord, and then we will be prepared to minister to others (2 Cor. 8:5). The Lord has equipped and enriched us in such a way that we can always have from him what we need when he calls us to help others. "And God is able to make all grace abound toward you, that you, always having all sufficiency in all things, may have an abundance for every good work" (9:8). When the Father sent Jesus, he gave us his very best. Why would he withhold anything else (Rom. 8:32)? "All things are yours" (1 Cor. 3:21), so we must ask the Father for what we need for assisting others. We are "poor, yet making many rich" (2 Cor. 6:10). "His divine power has given to us all things that pertain to life and godliness" (2 Pet. 1:3). It's not a matter of how poor we are in ourselves but how rich we are in Jesus.

There will be some surprises in heaven when people are rewarded by the Master for helping others and doing it for the sake of Jesus. He asks us, "What do you do more than others?" (Matt. 5:47), so let's not be like the priest and Levite and use other people for excuses. Jesus is our example and he will provide what we need when we need it. But first, let's give ourselves to the Lord, and then we will be ready to give to others.

> And remember the words of the Lord Jesus, that He said, "It is more blessed to give than to receive."
>
> Acts 20:35

21

But after I have been raised, *I will go before you*
to Galilee.

MATTHEW 26:32

It is one of the great encouragements of the Christian
life that Jesus goes before us. In Old Testament times,
God went before his people and led them through the
wilderness. After they entered the Promised Land, the Lord
led Joshua from one victory to another, and then led them
in dividing the land so that each tribe received its rightful
inheritance. The prophet Jeremiah said, "O LORD, I know
the way of man is not in himself; it is not in man who walks
to direct his own steps" (Jer. 10:23). Our enemy rejoices when
we lean on our own understanding and fail to seek the Lord's
direction (Prov. 3:5–6).

Jesus is our shepherd, and shepherds go before the flock
and lead them. (Cattlemen drive their steers from behind.)
"And when he brings out his own sheep, he goes before them;
and the sheep follow him, because they know his voice. Yet
they will by no means follow a stranger, but will flee from
him, for they do not know the voice of strangers. . . . My
sheep hear My voice, and I know them, and they follow Me"
(John 10:4–5, 27). How do we hear our Shepherd's voice? By
reading and hearing the Scriptures, by praying, and by being
sensitive to what the Spirit says to us through circumstances
and other Christians. I recall times when something a pastor
said in a Sunday message was just the word I needed. A true
Christian knows the voice of the Shepherd and is not led
astray by false teachers or counterfeit Christians.

Did you know that Jesus has gone before us to heaven
where he is preparing a home for each of his children? Jesus
the forerunner has gone behind the veil for us (Heb. 6:20).

The forerunner goes before to open the way for others to follow. On the annual Day of Atonement, the Jewish high priest went through the veil into the holy of holies to sprinkle the blood on the mercy seat, *but nobody followed him.* The next time Satan tells you that you will never make it to heaven, remind him that Jesus is already there. Tell him Jesus is the forerunner *and his people will follow him.* What is Jesus doing in heaven? As our Great High Priest, he is interceding for us at the throne of grace, where through him we can receive all the grace we need day after day. According to John 14:1–4, Christ is preparing a home in heaven for each believer, and we shall one day meet the Lord in the air and go with him to heaven.

Jesus goes before us whenever we are sent forth to serve him. "Follow Me, and I will make you fishers of men" (Matt. 4:19). The disciples who had been fishermen had caught living fish that subsequently died, but as "fishers of men" they would catch dead fish that would come alive! He prepares us for the service assigned to us and prepares the field where we will be serving. No matter how much training and experience we have, we always need the Lord's preparation for each ministry adventure.

John told Jesus that he and the other disciples had seen a man casting out demons, and they told him to stop because the man didn't follow the disciples (Mark 9:38–41). He forgot that every believer must follow Jesus and not follow the followers. "Imitate me," wrote Paul, "just as I also imitate Christ" (1 Cor. 11:1). Our responsibility is to follow Jesus and not to meddle with what he has planned for others (John 21:19–23). Keep your eyes of faith on Jesus, follow him and serve him, and all shall be well.

> If I go and prepare a place for you, I will come again and receive you to Myself, that where I am, there you may be also.
>
> John 14:3 NASB

22

And go quickly and tell His disciples that He is
risen from the dead.

Women were not considered reputable witnesses
in those days, but God chose women to be the
first witnesses that Jesus had risen from the dead.
The women had been the last to leave the cross and now were
the first to reach the tomb. They came early in the morning,
but a great day dawned before them!

A great earthquake (Matt. 28:2). God was still on the
throne, manifesting his power and fulfilling his promises.
Jesus had told his followers that he would rise from the dead
on the third day (16:21; 17:23; 20:19; 26:32), but somehow his
words had not penetrated their minds and hearts. Earthquakes
usually make us think of judgment, but this earthquake her-
alded the resurrection of the King. He who was despised was
now glorified and would ascend to heaven and be enthroned
with the Father. If that doesn't shake things, nothing will!

A great fear. The earthquake and the arrival of the angel
so frightened the Roman guards that they fainted dead away
(v. 4). What a marvelous opening for the resurrection drama.
All that Rome did to keep Jesus in the tomb was destroyed. The
angel broke the official Roman seal, moved the stone, and sat
on it, not to let Jesus out but to let the witnesses in. To those
who have trusted Christ as Savior and Lord, the empty tomb
cancels fear—fear of life, fear of death, fear of future judgment.
"Because I live," Jesus said, "you will live also" (John 14:19).

A great fact. "He is not here; for He is risen, as He said.
Come, see the place where the Lord lay" (Matt. 28:6). The
good news of salvation is that Christ died for our sins, was
buried and rose again from the dead on the third day (1 Cor.

15:1–4). After all, a dead Savior cannot give life to dead sinners. But he is alive! He showed himself alive to his followers (Acts 1:3) and made them witnesses of his resurrection (v. 22). Peter preached the resurrection to the Jews at Pentecost (2:32) and also to the crowd in the temple where he *proved* Jesus was alive by healing the lame beggar in Jesus's name (3:15). The apostles declared the resurrection of Jesus before the Jewish leaders who had bribed the Roman soldiers to say his body had been stolen at night (Matt. 28:11–15; Acts 5:27–32). We serve a living Savior!

A great privilege. The angel's "come and see" was followed by his "go quickly and tell" (Matt. 28:7). It was a "show and tell" situation: the angel showed them the empty tomb and told them to spread the word. The graveclothes that were wrapped around Christ's body lay there in the shape of the body *but were empty like a cocoon.* His living, glorious body had passed right through the fabric. But even more, the women met Jesus himself (vv. 9–10). It's good to have resurrection evidence on hand to confound the critics, but it's even better to have resurrection experience with the living Christ! With Paul, we say we want to "know Him and the power of His resurrection" (Phil. 3:10).

A great joy. The women loved Jesus and were thrilled to hear that he was alive and with them (Matt. 28:8). They knew that the resurrection meant that his sacrifice on the cross had been accepted by the Father and they had good news to proclaim: Satan had been defeated and death had been conquered! Jesus would promise them, "I am with you always, even to the end of the age" (v. 20). One of the best testimonies that Jesus is alive is the dedicated life of a joyful Christian who walks "in newness of life" (Rom. 6:4), because every day is resurrection day for those who have surrendered to him.

It's time to go and tell!

> How lovely on the mountains
> Are the feet of him who brings good news.
> > Isaiah 52:7 NASB

23

Jesus, moved with compassion, stretched out His
hand and touched him, and said to him, "*I am
willing; be cleansed.*"

MARK 1:41

Jesus had time for individuals and ministered personally
to people like Nicodemus the Pharisee, the woman at
the well of Sychar, the rich young ruler, the thief on the
cross, and here, a man full of leprosy (Luke 5:12). Leprosy
in that day was feared, and lepers were among the lowest
on the social ladder. They were required to stay six feet or
more away from other people, and when approaching others
had to cry out, "Unclean! Unclean!" Yet Jesus paused in his
busy schedule to listen to the man's plea, to speak to him, *to
touch him*, and to heal him. Jesus often spoke to huge crowds,
and many people who do that don't usually have time for
individuals, but Jesus was "moved with compassion" (*see*
Mark 6:34; 8:2). Let's take time for individuals, no matter
how full the schedule or how weary the body. This makes us
more like our Master.

Jesus met the physical needs of people as well as their
spiritual needs. He healed the sick and handicapped, fed the
hungry, and even raised the dead. He ministered to the whole
person, and this is the church's justification for founding
schools, hospitals, and other agencies that provide the needy
with the necessities of life. This man was desperate. He fell
on his face before Jesus, worshiped him, and implored him
to help him, and Jesus healed him. When you and I give to
agencies that minister to the body as well as proclaim the
gospel, we are following the example of our Lord.

What Jesus did for the man wasn't just in response to his
needs; he also responded to the man's faith. The leper knew

that Jesus could heal him; his only problem was whether Jesus was willing to heal him. The leper did not pray as the demonized boy's father prayed, "But if You can do anything, have compassion on us and help us" (Mark 9:22).

Prayer involves the will of God as well as the power of God. "Now this is the confidence that we have in Him, that if we ask anything according to His will, He hears us. And if we know that He hears us, whatever we ask, we know that we have the petitions that we have asked of Him" (1 John 5:14–15). But how can we know God's will? Our major guide is the Bible as the Spirit teaches us. This doesn't mean in desperation opening the Bible anywhere and pointing to a verse, but reading and meditating on the Scriptures daily and being attentive to God's voice. It means praying and waiting on the Lord, for sometimes he uses other believers to direct us. On more than one occasion, the Lord has given me guidance from a sentence in a sermon or even a casual remark in conversation. We must pray for the lost because we know the Lord wants them to be saved (1 Tim. 2:4; 2 Pet. 3:9).

Jesus told the man not to tell others who had healed him, but he disobeyed and spread the good news wherever he went. This meant Jesus had to "lay low" to escape the crowds and yet they seemed to find him. I'm sure the Lord forgave the man for disobeying orders; as Bishop Handley Moule said, "I would rather tone down a fanatic than try to resurrect a corpse." But the church today is just the opposite of this healed leper. Jesus told him to keep quiet but he told everybody; Jesus told us to tell everybody the gospel *and we keep quiet*. Which of us is the greater offender? If Jesus has done something special for you, tell somebody.

For we cannot but speak the things which we have seen and heard.

Acts 4:20

24

> He said to them, *"Take heed what you hear.* With the same measure you use, it will be measured to you; and to you who hear, more will be given."

MARK 4:24

In ancient times, most people didn't own copies of the Scriptures. However, they learned to listen with attention and remember the Scriptures as they were read or sung in the temple and the synagogue. People were better listeners and learners in those days. Today we have so many editions of the Bible available, including audio recordings and Braille editions, that we should know the Scriptures better than we do. But it isn't too late to get started reading God's Word systematically. After all, people take time to read novels and newspapers and to watch television, but they don't seem to have time for the Bible, the most important book ever published. Jesus warns us to exercise discernment in what we hear and see. Why?

What we choose to hear and see reveals what we are. The Scottish preacher George H. Morrison said, "Men hear with all that they have made themselves." Our appetite determines the menu we seek. If we know Jesus Christ and follow him, we will have an appetite for the truth as it is in Jesus and will daily spend time in the Scriptures. "But his delight is in the law of the LORD, and in His law he meditates day and night" (Ps. 1:2). Jesus compared the Word of God to seed (Luke 8:11), and seeds must be planted and watered before they can take root and bear fruit. The people who open their hearts and minds to the poisonous seeds of this world are planting lies where they should be planting God's truth. "Take heed what you hear!" (Mark 4:24).

What we choose to hear and see determines whether we gain or lose. In Scripture, the word *hear* carries with it the idea of obeying. It isn't enough just to read or hear the Bible; we must understand it and obey it. If we do, we grow in the knowledge of the Lord as well as in the graces of the Christian life. If we measure out time and energy to study the Word, God will measure out the blessing of the Spirit to us. The more we take in, the more the Lord will add to us every time we feed on God's truth. To waste time that could be devoted to the Word of God and prayer is to rob ourselves of spiritual riches. Paul told Timothy to exercise himself to godliness (1 Tim. 4:7). Nobody criticizes a person who follows a healthy exercise schedule, and God honors his children when they take time to be holy.

What we choose to hear and see determines how much we have to share with others. The measure we give to the Lord in our devotional exercises determines how much we will receive from him. The more we gratefully receive from God, the more he gives us; the more he gives us, the more we can share with others. The teacher, preacher, and Christian witness will always have spiritual treasures in their hearts to pass along to those in need. By exercising diligence and discernment, we reject the wisdom of the world and the lies of the devil and we help to nurture people in God's Word. If God's children would only feed on the milk, bread, meat, and honey of the Word, what a difference it would make in their lives and ministries!

> The soul of a lazy man desires, and has nothing;
> But the soul of the diligent shall be made rich.
>
> Proverbs 13:4

25

> *Then Peter took Him aside* and began to rebuke Him.
>
> MARK 8:32

Peter had just confessed that Jesus was the Christ, the Son of the living God. Knowing this, Peter should have been ready for the lessons Jesus wanted to teach the disciples about himself and the cross, but Peter was not ready. Because he was listening to Satan, Peter was opposing the will of God and therefore was rebuked by the Master. Instead of moving ahead spiritually, Peter went backward, which is the way Satan wants all of us to go.

Peter the follower tries to be a leader. Peter had been called to follow Jesus (Matt. 4:18–22), which meant to listen to his teaching, imitate his example, and obey his will. Instead, Peter acted like he knew more than Jesus knew and he tried to prevent his Master from obeying the Father. Peter was co-operating with Satan who had already made an offer to Jesus to forget the cross (4:9–11), and now Peter made the offer. The day would come when Peter would be a leader among the disciples, but he still had more growing to do. All leaders must first be listeners, learners, and followers. "Most assuredly, I say to you," Jesus told his disciples, "a servant is not greater than his master; nor is he who is sent greater than he who sent him" (John 13:16). "For who has known the mind of the LORD? Or who has become His counselor?" (Rom. 11:34). God does not need our advice. Our Lord gave us the best example when he prayed to the Father in the garden, "nevertheless not My will, but Yours, be done" (Luke 22:42).

Peter the rock becomes a stumbling block. At their first meeting with Jesus, Andrew introduced his brother to Jesus as Simon, but Jesus gave him the new name of *Peter*, a rock

(John 1:40–42; Matt. 16:18). Peter used this same image for all of God's people (1 Pet. 2:4). But when a rock is out of place, it becomes a stumbling block, and that's exactly what happened to Peter. Peter spoke privately to Jesus, but when Jesus rebuked him, he spoke for everyone to hear. The word *Satan* means "adversary," so Jesus was warning Peter that he was a traitor to his cause. This is a warning to us. One minute Peter gave a testimony that Jesus was the Son of God and the next minute he was speaking for the devil! This can happen to any child of God, so let's be careful to set our minds on things above and not on earthly things (Col. 3:1–3).

Peter moved from winning to losing. Not only would Jesus have a cross, but each follower of Jesus would have a cross. To carry a cross means to be headed for crucifixion. Each day we must willingly take up our cross and die to the old life. There are many ways to die, but *we cannot crucify ourselves.* All we can do is surrender and allow the Holy Spirit to identify us with the Master in his death (Gal. 2:20). Peter wanted Jesus to protect himself, to save himself from the pain and death he had announced. Jesus rebuked Peter for being selfish and worldly minded and warned all the disciples that it is only when we surrender to Christ and take our hands off that we save our lives and gain all he has for us. Our selfishness not only robs us but it also robs the people who need to hear the gospel.

Six days later, Jesus took Peter, James, and John to a high mountain and there revealed his glory (Mark 9:1–13). They moved from a lesson about suffering to a lesson about glory. We need not fear surrender for it leads to triumphant glory, and Peter got the message and passed it on to us (1 Pet. 1:6–8; 4:13–5:10; 2 Pet. 1:16–21). Don't fear the cross, for it leads to the crown. What seems to be loss will turn out to be glorious gain, both in this life and in the life to come.

> For whoever desires to save his life will lose it, but whoever loses his life for My sake and the gospel's will save it.
>
> Mark 8:35

26

Seeing from afar a fig tree having leaves, He went to see if perhaps He would find something on it. When He came to it, *He found nothing but leaves*, for it was not the season for figs.

MARK 11:13

When a fig tree has leaves, it's a sign that there are also figs, for the large leaves protect the fruit; but in this case, no figs had been produced at all. Jesus turned this event into an "action sermon" to teach some important lessons to his disciples and to us.

The first lesson has to do with the nation of Israel and *the importance of bearing fruit*. The Old Testament prophets used the fig tree and the vine as symbols of the nation of Israel. Jeremiah compared the sinful nation to rotten figs (Jer. 29:17), and Hosea wrote that, even though Israel was like "the firstfruits of the fig tree," their roots had dried up and they bore no fruit (Hos. 9:10, 16). During Joel's time, an invasion of locusts was ruining the nation, what God called "My vine" and "My fig tree" (Joel 1:7). The most common description of prosperity in Israel was to dwell under one's fig tree in peace and plenty (1 Kings 4:25; Micah 4:4). Prior to this event, Jesus had wept over the city of Jerusalem because Israel had an outward show of "religion" but had produced no fruit. Their worship was like this fig tree—nothing but leaves. Jesus told the hypocritical religious leaders, "Therefore I say to you, the kingdom of God will be taken from you and given to a nation bearing the fruits of it" (Matt. 21:43). I believe that "nation" is the church (1 Pet. 2:9), *but are we bearing fruit today*, or have our roots dried up, leaving us nothing but leaves?

Our Lord's second lesson has to do with *believing prayer*. The disciples heard him curse the fig tree, and the next morning as they walked to Jerusalem from Bethany, they saw that the tree had withered from the roots. Our Lord's response was, "Have faith in God" (Mark 11:22). He told them that their faith could move mountains, a vivid way of saying, "Faith accomplishes the impossible." Please keep in mind that when Jesus was ministering on earth, he lived by faith and not by his miraculous power. He prayed, he depended on the Holy Spirit, and he claimed the promises of God, just as we must do. I can never forget what Vance Havner said in a chapel message at seminary based on Hebrews 11:24–29, "Moses saw the invisible, Moses chose the imperishable, and Moses did the impossible." And so may we! During our years of ministry, my wife and I have seen God do great things because of the believing prayers of God's people. *Is the church today praying in faith and expecting God to do great things?*

The third lesson links with the second: as we pray, *we must be honest with God.* If there is anything in our hearts against anyone, our Father wants us to get that matter settled so he can answer our prayers. The religious leaders in Jerusalem were plotting to kill Jesus, yet they went right on in their religious duties with murder in their hearts! Jesus dealt with the topic of sin in the heart in Matthew 5:21–30, and we need to remember what he said. We must ask for forgiveness and then make things right with others, if we expect God to answer prayer. "If I regard iniquity in my heart, the Lord will not hear" (Ps. 66:18). "Above all else, guard your heart, for everything you do flows from it" (Prov. 4:23 TNIV).

Jesus is still seeking fruit. He has given us all that we need to have honest hearts and fruitful lives. Are we abiding in him, bearing fruit and moving mountains?

> Abide in Me, and I in you. As the branch cannot bear fruit of itself, unless it abides in the vine, neither can you, unless you abide in Me.
>
> John 15:4

27

It is like a man going to a far country, who left his house and gave authority to his servants, *and to each his work*, and commanded the doorkeeper to watch.

MARK 13:34

The Lord invented work and had Adam and Eve busy in the garden before paradise was lost. After their fall into sin, death entered the scene and work became toil. Our text gives us at least four instructions we must follow if our work is to be not a burden but a ministry for the Lord and a joy to our own hearts.

Accept your gifts and your work. Mature people accept themselves, their abilities and disabilities, and do the work God has called them to do. In his wisdom, the Lord prepares us for what he has prepared for us; if we allow him, he leads us to the places where our abilities are needed and where we can grow. Jesus compared working to eating. "My food is to do the will of Him who sent Me, and to finish His work" (John 4:34). When the work and the worker are matched, work is nourishment, not punishment. Work is God's gift, and workers compete with themselves and not with one another. All of us labor for the Lord and want him glorified.

Serve the Lord faithfully from your heart. Paul admonished Christian servants and masters to remember that they both had a Master in heaven, Jesus Christ their Savior and Lord (Eph. 6:5–9). Jesus ministers to his church constantly at the throne of grace in heaven and we can go to him at any time to receive the grace we need (Heb. 4:14–16). We are to serve our employers as though we are serving Christ, which means giving our very best. Our employers and co-workers look on the outward appearance, but God looks on the heart (1 Sam.

16:7). He sees our motives and knows if we are cutting corners. The Lord is not a difficult taskmaster, nor does he ever permit us to have tasks we are unable to handle successfully. His yoke is easy and his burden is light (Matt. 11:28–30).

Finish the tasks he gives you, and finish well. In his high priestly prayer, Jesus said to his Father, "I have glorified You on the earth. I have finished the work which You have given Me to do" (John 17:4). "It is finished!" he shouted from the cross, and then gave up his spirit (19:30). Moses finished building the tabernacle (Exod. 40:33) and Solomon the building of the temple (1 Kings 6:9). In his second letter to Timothy, Paul wrote, "I have fought the good fight, I have finished the race, I have kept the faith" (2 Tim. 4:7). All of us should be praying, "Lord, help me to end well," as Paul encouraged his associate Archippus (Col. 4:17). Too many people make good beginnings but fail to end well.

Live expectantly. No one knows the day or the hour of our Lord's return and it's important to have expectant hearts that say, "Perhaps today!" Jesus commanded us to watch, which doesn't mean to stand gazing up at the heavens (Acts 1:4–8) but to stay awake and be spiritually alert. Our attitude should not be negative: at last we will be delivered from the world and relieved of our problems. It should be positive: we will see Jesus and become like him!

Know what your gifts are and what your work is, and do your best to please the Lord. That responsibility is for all believers, not just for "full-time Christian workers."

And what I say to you, I say to all: Watch!

Mark 13:37

28

Then He said to them, *"My soul is exceedingly sorrowful, even to death. Stay here and watch."*

MARK 14:34

Tour guides in Jerusalem may show you three different sites on the Mount of Olives where Jesus met with his disciples. Which one, if any, is the genuine one? That is not important. We are not interested in geography but theology. A better question is: What was Jesus doing there and what does it mean to the church today? Three images in the text help to answer those questions.

The first image is that of *a garden*. Jesus was on his way to Calvary to die for the sins of the world, and sin first entered the human race in a garden (Gen. 3). God had provided our first parents with everything they needed for life and happiness; all they had to do was obey his will. But the first Adam disobeyed God and plunged the human race into sin and death, while the last Adam, Jesus Christ, was "obedient to the point of death, even the death of the cross" (Phil. 2:8; 1 Cor. 15:45). Jesus was buried in a tomb in a garden, not far from where he died (John 19:41–42).

But the garden where he prayed was called "Gethsemane," which means "olive press," and that speaks of suffering. "My heart is breaking, it almost kills me," reads the Charles B. Williams translation of Mark 14:34. Heaven is a "garden city," but had Jesus not experienced Gethsemane and Calvary, we would have no access to heaven.

This leads us to the second image—*the cup*. In Scripture, drinking from a cup means accepting what has been ordained for you. Sometimes it is a cup of blessing and other times a cup of sorrow or even judgment. The cup the Father prepared was for Jesus a cup of agony, but for those who have trusted him, a cup of salvation and blessing. Jesus prayed that, if it were possible, the Father would remove the cup from him, but he added "nevertheless, not what I will, but what You will" (Mark 14:36). No matter what was in the cup, it was mixed by the Father and Jesus willingly drank it. He knew that the prophet Isaiah had predicted the sorrows of his life and death: "He is despised and rejected by men, a Man of sorrows and acquainted with grief" (Isa. 53:3). Jesus did experience joy (Luke 10:21), but his life was predominantly one of pain and sorrow, especially during his arrest and his six hours on the cross. He not only experienced sorrows but he carried our sorrows to the cross. "Surely He has borne our griefs and carried our sorrows" (Isa. 53:4). Any cup that we must drink he has already drunk, and can give us the grace we need to go from suffering to glory and from the cross to the crown. "In the world you will have tribulation; but be of good cheer, I have overcome the world" (John 16:33). We are those who are "sorrowful, yet always rejoicing" (2 Cor. 6:10).

The third image is *sleep*. Jesus took Peter, James, and John with him to the place of prayer, but instead of encouraging him in his trials, they went to sleep! Sleep in Scripture is one picture of spiritual lethargy. "Therefore let us not sleep, as others do, but let us watch and be sober" (1 Thess. 5:6). "And do this, knowing the time, that now it is high time to awake out of sleep" (Rom. 13:11). There is a desperate need for spiritual vigor and alertness in the church today. We lack the excitement and enablement of the early church; we need to be filled with the Spirit and to focus on "prayer and . . . the ministry of the word" (Acts 6:4). Jesus is interceding for us in heaven while we are sleeping here on earth. It's one thing to have spiritual rest and quite something else to suffer from spiritual lethargy.

> Watch therefore, for you do not know when the master of the house is coming—in the evening, at midnight, at the crowing of the rooster, or in the morning—lest, coming suddenly, he find you sleeping.
>
> Mark 13:35–36

29

> *But Jesus still answered nothing*, so that Pilate
> marveled.
>
> MARK 15:5

To everything there is a season," King Solomon wrote, "a time for every purpose under heaven," and he included in his list "a time to keep silence, and a time to speak" (Eccles. 3:1, 7).

Most of us can recall times when we should have spoken up and did not and also times when we should have kept quiet but spoke up. Jesus knew how to handle both of these disciplines, and we clearly see him doing it during his so-called trials after his arrest.

Jesus was silent before his accusers. The Jewish religious leaders—the chief priests, the elders, scribes, and council—were determined to kill Jesus and even enlisted false witnesses to strengthen their case. These same people accused Jesus when he stood before Pilate, but he did not answer the accusers or defend himself. When the high priest put Jesus under oath, he admitted that he was indeed the Son of God (Matt. 26:62–64), but he never responded to the accusations of the leaders. This fulfilled the prophecy of Isaiah, "He was oppressed and He was afflicted, yet He opened not His mouth; He was led as a lamb to the slaughter, and as a sheep before its shearers is silent, so He opened not His mouth" (Isa. 53:7). "And while He was being accused by the chief priests and elders, He answered nothing" (Matt. 27:12). The Good Shepherd was being treated like a lamb in the slaughterhouse. In a few hours, he would lay down his life for the sheep. All who follow Jesus will on some occasion be falsely accused even as he was; like he did, let's allow God to control our speech and bless our silence.

Jesus was silent before King Herod (Luke 23:6–12). Pilate the politician, trying to escape making a decision about Jesus, sent him to Herod Antipas, the man who had ordered the execution of John the Baptist. Herod was anxious to meet Jesus and hoped to see him do a miracle, but Jesus said nothing to Herod and did nothing for Herod. Jesus was not a religious entertainer. *When Herod had killed John the Baptist, he had silenced the voice of God.* Herod had listened to John speak but had not obeyed the Word of God, and according to King David, when God keeps silence, it's like our going down into the pit of death (Ps. 28:1). God's Word is alive and powerful (Heb. 4:12), and if we believe and obey, it imparts life, but if we reject it, it brings death. Moses and Aaron brought God's living Word to Pharaoh in Egypt, but he would not listen; death came to the land. We who are children of God must obey him, or he may not speak to us and our sin will "kill" our witness and our service, and, if we don't repent, may also kill us. "There is sin leading to death" (1 John 5:16).

Jesus was silent before Pilate (John 19:9). Yes, Jesus answered some of Pilate's questions, but when asked, "Where are you from?" Jesus gave no reply. The thing that frightened Pilate was our Lord's claim that he was the Son of God, the Ruler over a special kingdom. Pilate was a good politician but a poor theologian, and could not understand that Jesus ruled over a spiritual kingdom that came from heaven, a kingdom that one day would destroy the Roman Empire. Rome succeeded by murder, lies, and oppressive authority, but Jesus ruled through life, truth, and loving authority. Like most world leaders today, Pilate could not understand that at all.

Through his Word and by his Spirit, God is speaking to his church today. Are we listening? "He who has an ear, let him hear what the Spirit says to the churches" is found seven times in the last book of the Bible!

My soul, wait silently for God alone.

Psalm 62:5

30

And having come in, the angel said to her, "Rejoice, highly favored one, the Lord is with you; *blessed are you among women.*"

LUKE 1:28

I n the original Greek text of the New Testament, the word translated "highly favored" is found only here and in Ephesians 1:6, "to the praise of the glory of His grace, by which He made us accepted [highly favored] in the Beloved." We don't receive God's grace because we deserve it but because in his love he grants it to us. In Jesus Christ, every believer has been "highly favored" by the Lord. The Father has "blessed us with every spiritual blessing in the heavenly places in Christ" (1:3). What did this mean in Mary's life, and what does it mean in our lives?

To begin with, it means *salvation.* Mary rejoiced in God her Savior (Luke 1:46–47). We cannot be saved by our good works, because the only way to be saved is by faith in Jesus Christ (Eph. 2:8–9). It is the grace of God that brings salvation to us (Titus 2:11). Mary didn't praise Moses or the laws of Moses, for nobody can be saved by keeping the law (Gal. 2:16; 3:11). Even though Mary was the human channel by which the Son of God came into the world, she needed to have a Savior.

Grace also fills us with *joy.* Being a virgin, Mary realized that bearing a child would elicit all sorts of responses from the people in Nazareth where she lived. But she was willing to bear that pain so that she might fulfill the will of God. "Behold the maidservant of the Lord!" Mary said to the angel. "Let it be to me according to your word" (Luke 1:38). Surrendering to the Lord is an act of faith that brings deep joy into the heart. Mary's song of praise (vv. 46–55) reminds us of Hannah's song of praise in 1 Samuel 2:1–10, and it's likely Mary knew Hannah's song. If we are going to submit to the Lord and sing about it, we need grace in our hearts (Col. 3:16).

Mary would suffer in years to come, and it takes grace to suffer for the Lord and glorify him. "My grace is sufficient for you," the Lord told Paul, "for My strength is made perfect in weakness" (2 Cor. 12:9). When Mary and Joseph took the child Jesus to the temple to present him to the Lord, Simeon told her that a sword would pierce through her own soul (Luke 2:25–35), and it did. Mary stood at the cross with John, and Jesus commissioned John to care for her (John 19:25–27). As his mother, Mary was the only person in all Jerusalem who could have rescued Jesus from the cross, but she kept silent because she knew the cross was in the plan of God. There may be times in our lives when everything appears to be against us, but those are the times when God's inexhaustible grace enables us to keep going and, like Mary, praise God for the privilege.

God's grace gave Mary a *spiritual family*, for we find her with the brothers and sisters in the upper room, awaiting the coming of the Holy Spirit (Acts 1:12–14). They were not praying to her; she was praying to the Lord with them. Not only was the infant church praying but Peter was opening the Scriptures to them and preparing them for Pentecost, and Mary needed the Holy Spirit just as much as the others. We all need a church family. Yes, no church is perfect just as no family is perfect, but we still love one another, pray for one another, and encourage one another.

The last recorded words of Mary in Scripture are in John 2:5, when she said to the servants at the wedding, "Whatever He says to you, do it." That is good counsel! If each day we would read the Scriptures and obey what God says to us, what a difference it would make!

Like Mary, we are "highly favored—highly graced" by God (Luke 1:28). Does it show?

31

Blessed is she who believed, for there will be a fulfillment of those things which were told her from the Lord.

LUKE 1:45

These words were spoken to Mary by Elizabeth, who in spite of her great age was pregnant with John the Baptist. God was doing great things for both of these women. God had announced great things to Mary and would do great things for her, not because she herself was great but because she put her faith in the true and living God who alone is great. How wonderful it would be if every Christian today would surrender to the Lord as Mary did (Luke 1:38). Then the Lord would do the "greater works" Jesus promised his church (John 14:12–14), and the unbelieving world would sit up and take notice. If we truly want to see "greater works" in our lives we must follow the example of Mary.

There is grace to receive. Whenever God wants to do something great in and through one of his children, he always begins with grace. He called the aged Abraham and Sarah to found the Jewish nation and in his grace gave them a son. He chose Moses to lead his people from Egypt to the Promised Land and graciously equipped him to do the job. He called Joshua to claim the Promised Land for Israel and gave him the grace he needed to defeat every enemy. God's calling always includes his equipping and enabling, if we surrender to him and walk by faith. "He who has begun a good work in you will complete it until the day of Jesus Christ" (Phil. 1:6). If you are chosen by God to serve in some way, and you feel inadequate, that is a good sign! Just say with Paul, "For when I am weak, then I am strong" (2 Cor. 12:10). The servant who feels adequate will fail; the servant who feels inadequate will glorify God. "My grace is sufficient for you, for My strength is made perfect in weakness" (v. 9).

There is a promise to believe. We do not live on explanations; we live on promises. Dr. Bob Cook used to remind us, "If you can explain what's going on, God didn't do it." Elizabeth's husband, Zacharias, did not believe God's promise and was mute until his son was born (Luke 1:18–20). Mary's song of praise reveals that she knew the Old Testament Scriptures, especially Hannah's praise song in 1 Samuel 2:1–11, for "faith comes by hearing, and hearing by the word of God" (Rom. 10:17). "I used to think that I should close my Bible and pray for faith," said evangelist D. L. Moody, "but I came to see that it was from studying the Word that I was to get faith." So let's pray for faith and then open the Bible! When the Lord wants us to do something, he always gives us a promise from Scripture that will carry us through.

There is a purpose to achieve. Elizabeth said there would be a fulfillment of all God said he would do—and there was! The Lord told Mary that her Son would be the Savior (*Jesus* means "savior") and the King (Luke 1:31–33), and God kept his word. "There has not failed one word of all His good promise," said King Solomon (1 Kings 8:56). It has often been said that the Lord is not looking for better methods but for better men and women of faith. In Christian living and serving, it is faith that makes the difference, for "the just shall live by his faith" (Hab. 2:4). What God calls us to do may look impossible, but as the angel Gabriel told Mary, "For with God nothing will be impossible" (Luke 1:37). First Mary surrendered to the Lord (v. 38), experienced God's grace, and claimed God's promise. Then she rejoiced in the Lord, and so may we. "Then they believed His words; they sang His praise" (Ps. 106:12). Blessed are those who believe!

> No one is holy like the LORD,
> For there is none besides You,
> Nor is there any rock like our God.
>
> 1 Samuel 2:2

32

He will thoroughly clean out His threshing floor,
and gather the wheat into His barn; but *the chaff
He will burn* with unquenchable fire.

John the Baptist was not a "reed shaken by the wind" (Matt. 11:7), for he was preparing people to welcome their Savior. That is the most serious decision anyone can make because it determines our eternal destiny. "Behold! The Lamb of God who takes away the sin of the world," John shouted (John 1:29). "He must increase, but I must decrease" (3:30). John even dared to preach about hell. He saw a harvest coming when God would separate the wheat from the chaff and burn the chaff in unquenchable fire. God did not prepare hell for people but for Satan and his angels (Matt. 25:41), and for those who reject Christ and choose Satan. What should be the Christian's response to the fact of hell and the certainty of eternal judgment?

Our first response should be that of *gratitude in our worship*, for who are we that we should be saved from the wrath of God? Certainly we did not deserve to be brought into the family of God, for we were born sinners, we lived as sinners, and we even loved to sin. Yet God the Father chose us; God the Son died for us; and God the Spirit convicted us, brought us to faith in Christ, and sealed us for eternity (Eph. 1:3–14). We had done nothing to deserve forgiveness, yet God loves us, forgives us, and showers us with blessings! Jesus intercedes for us in heaven and the Spirit lives within us. It is grace from beginning to end and it still amazes me. When we lose the wonder of salvation, we take the first step toward sin. Charles Wesley said it best: "Amazing love / how can it be? / That thou, my God / Shouldst die for me."

Our second response should be that of *compassion in our witness*. The apostle Paul had "great sorrow and continual grief" in his heart because of his burden for the lost people of Israel. He was even willing to go to hell himself if it would mean the salvation of the Jews (Rom. 9:1–5). This reminds us of Moses, who was willing to die on behalf of his people who had sinned (Exod. 32:31–35). Both Moses and Paul (Rom. 10:1) interceded for their people, and we, too, should pray for the salvation of the lost. God has no pleasure in the death of the wicked (Ezek. 18:23, 32; 33:11). He is not willing that any should perish (2 Pet. 3:9), but "desires all men to be saved and to come to the knowledge of the truth" (1 Tim. 2:4). We are here on earth, not to be judges or prosecuting attorneys condemning lost people, but to be witnesses pointing to Jesus and sharing the good news of the gospel. Do you have a list of the names of people for whom you pray?

Our third response should be that of *obedience in our walk*. Our task is not to ask, "Lord, are there few who are saved?" (Luke 13:23), but to be sure that we are saved and that we live like it. "The secret things belong to the LORD our God, but those things which are revealed belong to us and to our children forever, that we may do all the words of this law" (Deut. 29:29). Our godly lives may be the only versions of the Bible the unsaved will ever read. Let's not waste time and energy debating the fine points of theology when the world is filled with people who know nothing about the simple plan of salvation. Let your light shine in this dark world.

We may not like the truth about hell, but the same Bible that assures believers they are going to heaven (John 14:1–6) also assures unbelievers they are going to hell—unless they receive Jesus Christ into their hearts (3:14–21). What are we doing about it?

> Jesus said to him, "I am the way, the truth, and the life. No one comes to the Father except through Me."
>
> John 14:6

33

> When He saw their faith, He said to him, "Man, *your sins are forgiven you."*

LUKE 5:20

Jesus was very popular during the first year of his ministry and great crowds followed him. Suppose you and I had been in Capernaum and pushed our way into that crowded house? What would we have learned about Jesus?

Jesus is a teacher. The people had different motives for crowding into the house. Some were just curious to see this "celebrity" up close and hear what he had to say. Others were seeking truth, or perhaps healing, and hoped he could help them. Some, like the scribes and Pharisees, came with a critical spirit and hoped to find fault. Luke tells us that Jesus was teaching (5:17) and Mark says that he was preaching (2:2), so there was both explanation and application in his ministry. If we come to Jesus with a prepared heart, we can learn from him; if we go away and obey what we heard, the blessing will be even greater. "Blessed are those who hunger and thirst for righteousness, for they shall be filled" (Matt. 5:6). Listen to Jesus and learn.

Jesus is a healer. Luke tells us that "the power of the Lord was present to heal them" (5:17). This means there were people present who had faith, for in Nazareth he could not do many mighty works because of their unbelief (Matt. 13:58). When we go to a church gathering to worship, do we have a believing heart that enables the Spirit to work, or a critical heart that grieves the Holy Spirit? One man's healing in particular is described, a paralytic who was carried to the house and let down through the roof. Praise God for believing people who have a concern for others and let nothing stand in their way! Crowds are good, but if they keep needy people from getting to Jesus, they are a hindrance. Zacchaeus the tax collector also faced that problem (Luke 19:1–10). Our Lord's miracles were not only gracious acts of kindness but also "action sermons" that taught spiritual lessons. Sin is like sickness (Isa. 1:4–6). It starts small and gradually grows so that it controls the victim's life, and if not cured it results in death. In the text we are now studying, Jesus connected sin and sickness; it's possible that this man was paralyzed because he indulged in sin.

Jesus is the Savior. Our text records the first thing Jesus said to the man was that his sins were forgiven. To make a man healthy but not change his heart would only make him a healthy sinner! The basic problem would not be solved. People who have sinned against each other can forgive each other, but only God can completely cleanse a sinful heart and wipe the record clean. Forgiveness means pardon and deliverance from bondage and guilt of sin. When our Lord said this, he offended the religious leaders who were present because they didn't believe he was really the Son of God. It was easy for Jesus to speak these words, but behind them was his sacrifice on the cross. "Surely He has borne our griefs and carried our sorrows . . . and by His stripes we are healed" (Isa. 53:4–5). Jesus healed the man's body as proof that he had also forgiven his sins. You can't see the heart but you can see the transformed body.

Jesus said "Your sins are forgiven you" to the paralytic and also to a sinful woman who wept at his feet (Luke 7:36–50). *But he has also said it to all who have trusted him as Savior!* "I write to you, little children, because your sins are forgiven you for His name's sake" (1 John 2:12). The verb "forgiven" is in the perfect tense: you have been forgiven, you are forgiven, and you always will be forgiven. If that isn't good news, what is?

> He was wounded for our transgressions,
> He was bruised for our iniquities;
> The chastisement for our peace was upon Him,
> And by His stripes we are healed.
>
> Isaiah 53:5

34

Bless those who curse you, and pray for those who spitefully use you.

LUKE 6:28

The scribes and Pharisees taught that "love your neighbor" in Leviticus 19:18 meant "love your *Jewish* neighbor," and then they added, "and hate the Gentiles." But that is not what Moses wrote, nor is it what Jesus taught in the Sermon on the Mount or the parable of the Good Samaritan (Luke 10:25–37). When it comes to enemies, keep in mind three basic truths.

If we are obedient Christians, we will have enemies. If we live godly lives and stand up for what is right, somebody is likely to oppose us. Jesus said, "Blessed are those who are persecuted for righteousness' sake, for theirs is the kingdom of heaven" (Matt. 5:10). He told his disciples, "If you were of the world, the world would love its own. Yet because you are not of the world, but I chose you out of the world, therefore the world hates you" (John 15:19). Paul wrote, "Yes, and all who desire to live godly in Christ Jesus will suffer persecution" (2 Tim. 3:12). He told the Philippian believers, "For to you it has been granted on behalf of Christ, not only to believe in Him, but also to suffer for His sake" (Phil. 1:29). Jesus lived a perfect life and never harmed a single person, yet he was hated by the religious crowd and crucified. God's people are salt in a decaying world and light in a darkening world—and salt stings and light exposes. The world likes a compromising Christian, but a compromising Christian won't get much of a reward.

If we are obedient Christians, we will not declare war on others. I can't help it if there are people who don't like me and want to hurt me, but I *can* help it if I try to hurt them.

72

Unconverted people can return evil for evil and good for good because that's the way humans act. To return evil for good is acting like the devil, but to return good for evil is acting like Jesus, and he is our supreme example. "Love your enemies" (Luke 6:27) doesn't mean I have to like them, but only that I treat them the way my heavenly Father treats me. He is patient with me, he forgives me, he wants the best for me, and he always gives me another chance to do better. If I truly love my enemies for Jesus's sake, I will return good for evil, I will bless them even though they curse me, and I will pray for them (vv. 27–28). To "bless" others is to want God's best for them and to ask God to show his gracious kindness to them. There are times when we feel like praying one of the imprecatory psalms; but according to Romans 12:9–21, judgment doesn't belong to us but to the Lord. Jesus prayed for his enemies (Luke 23:34) and so did Stephen (Acts 7:59–60).

If we are obedient Christians, God will help us overcome. "If it is possible, as much as depends on you, live peaceably with all men" (Rom. 12:18). Sometimes it is not possible and everything we attempt seems to fail. *But don't quit.* Keep loving, praying, and doing good, and leave the results with the Lord. God the Father is for you and will not abandon you. "Therefore let those who suffer according to the will of God commit their souls to Him in doing good, as to a faithful Creator" (1 Pet. 4:19). God the Son is with you as you share in "the fellowship of His sufferings" (Phil. 3:10). He has won victory over the world (John 16:33). And God the Holy Spirit is with you to rest upon you and bring glory to God (1 Pet. 4:14). The Lord can turn curses into blessings (Deut. 23:5; Neh. 13:2) and he can use our blessings to defuse the enemy's curses.

But he gives us more grace.

James 4:6 TNIV

35

You gave Me no kiss, but this woman has not ceased to kiss My feet since the time I came in.

LUKE 7:45

A n insincere invitation. Simon the Pharisee asked Jesus to dine at his house, and Jesus accepted the invitation. It's interesting how much ministry Jesus was able to have with people as he ate with them at the table, even those who opposed him. He knew that Simon's purpose was insincere, for the Pharisees were constantly looking for opportunities to criticize Jesus and get him into trouble with the religious leaders. Simon proved his insincerity by the way he treated Jesus. He did not welcome Jesus with a kiss, he did not anoint his head with perfumed oil, and he did not provide water for washing his feet. Four times in Matthew 23, Jesus called the Pharisees blind (vv. 16–17, 24, 26), and the word certainly applied to Simon. He was blind to his own sins, he was blind to the remarkable transformation of the woman, and he was blind to the person of Jesus Christ. Yet he invited Jesus to his table! Jesus accepted, not for his own good but for the good of Simon. Sometimes we have to go to dinners only for the good of others.

A surprising interruption. When the woman came into the banquet hall, Simon must have been terribly embarrassed. Simon was a self-righteous man whose heart had never broken over his sins nor had he ever experienced the kind of repentance and love demonstrated by this woman. He was religious, but it was only playacting, keeping up appearances. The woman had been guilty of sins of the flesh, but Simon was guilty of sins of the spirit (2 Cor. 7:1). She had been a prodigal daughter, but Simon was an elder brother who knew how to criticize others but not how to forgive them (Luke 15:25–32).

The woman did not come hoping to get some food; she came to pour out her love to Jesus. If you check a harmony of the Gospels, you will find that many Bible students think she had trusted Christ when he spoke that gracious invitation recorded in Matthew 11:28–30, "Come to Me, all you who labor and are heaven laden, and I will give you rest. Take My yoke upon you and learn from Me, for I am gentle and lowly in heart, and you will find rest for your souls. For My yoke is easy and My burden is light." Everything the woman did to Jesus, Simon had neglected to do. There are sins of omission as well as sins of commission. She washed his feet with her tears, wiped them with her hair, kissed them, and poured expensive ointment on them. This was her way of saying that Jesus was her Savior and Lord, that she had heard and believed his invitation and had found rest.

An embarrassing revelation. Jesus knew what Simon was thinking, so he told him a parable and rebuked him for his unkind thoughts. The Good Shepherd always defends his sheep (Rom. 8:31–34). He openly told Simon and his guests how the host had treated him, and Simon could not deny it. Would we want our sins announced at the next church banquet? Probably not, but God already knows them.

A gracious benediction. Jesus said to the woman, "Your sins are forgiven. Your faith has saved you. Go in peace" (Luke 7:48, 50). It was not her expensive gift or her tears that saved her, but her faith in the Savior. Everything she had done to Jesus only revealed that she had repented of all her sins and trusted Christ, and now she loved him and wanted to thank him. Faith brings salvation and salvation brings peace.

Faith, peace, love, and tears. Has this been *your* experience?

Therefore, having been justified by faith, we have peace with God through our Lord Jesus Christ . . . because the love of God has been poured out in our hearts.

Romans 5:1, 5

36

"Return to your own house, and tell what great things God has done for you." And he went his way and proclaimed throughout the whole city what great things Jesus had done for him.

LUKE 8:39

There are five prayers in this remarkable event in the cemetery, three from the demons (Luke 8:28, 31, 32), one from the local residents (v. 37), and one from the healed demoniac (v. 38). The demons got what they asked for and so did the residents, but not the healed demoniac, and his request was a good one. All he wanted to do was go with Jesus, but Jesus told him to go home and tell everybody what the Lord had done for him. It's clear that he was a new man, for he was clothed, sitting at the feet of Jesus, and in his right mind. Why, then, didn't Jesus grant his request and allow him to be one of his personal followers?

To begin with, Jesus didn't "exhibit" new believers like entertainers at a sideshow. A few years ago, there was an epidemic of so-called celebrity conversions in the United States, the thrust of which was "you should trust Christ because these famous people have trusted Christ." A. W. Tozer called this "the Wheaties approach to evangelism" because celebrities, especially winning athletes, were often pictured on cereal boxes. But sinners should turn to Christ no matter what the famous people might do, and the fact that they are rich and famous is a guarantee of nothing. Paul reminded us that "not many mighty, not many noble, are called" (1 Cor. 1:26). I have personally met some of these people and they gave every evidence that their salvation was genuine, but, sad to say, many others have fallen by the wayside and been forgotten. Note that Paul wrote "many," not "any." The rich and famous are saved by that letter *m*!

Jesus sent the man home because the people there knew him best and his testimony would have a greater impact. They knew the sad history of his becoming demonized, the reality of it and the agony of it, and they would have to admit that he was a different man. It's interesting that Jesus told the healed leper not to say anything to anybody (Mark 1:43) but commanded the healed demoniac to tell everybody. The word translated "proclaimed" in our text refers to the pronouncements of the herald of a king. Jesus had commissioned him to carry the good news and he obeyed. Would that more of us followed his example!

This leads to a third reason he was sent home: he may have had some damage to repair. Was he married? Did he have a family? Or was he living with his parents? The way he behaved at home and the way he left home (or was asked to leave) may have hurt family relationships, and the Lord would help him make things right. One of our first responsibilities after trusting Christ is to "mend fences," or perhaps "take down fences."

I'm sure the Lord arranged for believers in his neighborhood to help him feed on God's truth and grow in grace. Every new Christian needs to fellowship with other believers who can explain the basics of the Christian life. I recall a well-known Midwest singer who phoned to tell me he had trusted Christ. "What do I do next?" he asked. We met for lunch and I urged him to get into a good church and have the pastor involve him in a discipleship program. Instead, he started a new organization, made recordings of his new songs, and went from performance to performance—but never developed spiritually. Then he passed from the scene and we never saw him again, though I tried to locate him. I wish he had heeded my advice.

Let them first learn to show piety at home.

1 Timothy 5:4

37

Now it came to pass, when the time had come for
Him to be received up, that *He steadfastly set His
face* to go to Jerusalem.

LUKE 9:51

Many people wander their way through life when they should be marching on God's path and moving toward the goal he has chosen for them. These wanderers lack both purposeful goals and godly determination. They need "steadfastness," a quality of character possessed by the early church. "And they continued steadfastly in the apostles' doctrine and fellowship, in the breaking of bread, and in prayers" (Acts 2:42). Their hope in Jesus was as steadfast and secure as an anchor (Heb. 6:19), and they stood fast in the gospel and in the faith (1 Cor. 15:1–5; 16:13). When it comes to dedication and determination, Jesus is our example.

Jesus walked on *an appointed path*. This was prophesied in Isaiah 50:7, "For the Lord GOD will help me; therefore I will not be disgraced; therefore I have set My face like a flint, and I know that I will not be ashamed." Everything about our Lord's earthly ministry was planned, from the time of his birth (Gal. 4:4–5) to the day of his death (1 Cor. 5:7). In the Gospel of John, you often meet the phrases "his hour" or "the hour," referring to the hour of Jesus's death (2:4; 7:6, 8, 30; 8:20; 12:23; 13:1; 16:32; 17:1). The place of his death would be the holy city of Jerusalem, "for it cannot be that a prophet should perish outside of Jerusalem" (Luke 13:33). How he would die is revealed in Psalm 22, and why he would die is explained in Isaiah 53. During the years of my life and ministry, I have leaned heavily on my life verse, Psalm 16:11, "You will show me the path of life; in Your presence is fullness of joy; at Your right hand are pleasures forevermore." Each of us has an appointed path; each of us has a Jerusalem.

Jesus walked on *a difficult path*. No sooner had he launched his ministry by being baptized by John than he was driven into the wilderness to confront Satan (Mark 1:12). Satan's final temptation was to offer him all the kingdoms of the world if he would bow down and worship him (Matt. 4:8–11). This was an attempt to detour Jesus from the cross, but our Lord said, "No!" The devil even used Peter to tempt him away from the cross (16:21–23). After he had fed the five thousand, the crowd wanted to make him king (John 6:14–15). It was another detour. But Jesus steadfastly held to the Father's will and, knowing what lay before him, kept journeying toward Jerusalem. It was George Washington Carver who said that people should be judged not only by the positions they hold but also by the obstacles they had to overcome to get there.

Jesus walked on *a triumphant way*. Before going to Gethsemane, he said to his Father, "I have glorified You on the earth. I have finished the work which You have given Me to do" (17:4). I hope I can honestly say that when I come to the end of my assigned path. The cross looked like defeat, but it was actually victory. His nation rejected him, the religious leaders hated him, his treasurer betrayed him, his disciples abandoned him and fled, and even the Father forsook him at that crucial moment when our sins were laid on him. Yet Jesus was faithful to the end and could cry out, "It is finished!" He anticipated the joy that was set before him in glorifying the Father and sharing that glory with his church (John 17:24; Heb. 12:1–2; Jude 24). Who can mind the journey when the road leads Home?

> However, I consider my life worth nothing to me; my only aim is to finish the race and complete the task the Lord Jesus has given me—the task of testifying to the good news of God's grace.
>
> Acts 20:24 TNIV

38

> Then He said to them, "The harvest truly is great,
> *but the laborers are few*; therefore pray the Lord of
> the harvest to send out laborers into His harvest."
>
> LUKE 10:2

Why are there so few laborers? Is Jesus such a cruel master that nobody can work for him or with him? Was Paul in error when he wrote, "For we are God's fellow workers" (1 Cor. 3:9)? Is the harvest so unimportant that the church can afford to ignore it? The spectators are not few, nor are the critics and the sidewalk superintendents; but to enlist sowers and waterers and harvesters and binders is not an easy task.

One reason for the lack of laborers is that many of God's people can't see. God's people are blind and don't notice the ripened fields or the missing workers. They aren't obeying the command of Jesus, "Behold, I say to you, lift up your eyes and look at the fields, for they are already white for harvest" (John 4:35). What we see with our eyes is largely determined by what we love in our hearts. "And when Jesus went out He saw a great multitude; and He was moved with compassion for them, and healed their sick" (Matt. 14:14). Others are laboring and we are criticizing. Shame on us! Do we have compassion?

To blindness we must add selfishness. Our text is preceded by Luke 9:57–62, so take time to read that brief but moving paragraph. Here are three men—two volunteers and one who was drafted—and none of them ended up laboring in the harvest fields. The first man would not deny himself. He wanted a comfortable home and a warm bed, but Jesus didn't write that into the contract. Jesus didn't have a cozy home or a warm bed in his own contract! The second man would not take up his cross and die to the normal pressures of this world. Certainly we should love and respect our parents, but if that love keeps us from obeying God's call, that love is wrong. Didn't Jesus leave the heavenly Father to come to earth to die for us? The third man had his own agenda and had to attend a farewell party at home. That little phrase "me first" says a lot (v. 61). Jesus warned him against looking back while trying to plow the field. *How could he follow Jesus and look back at the same time?* Paul made it clear that there was one thing he did: "forgetting those things which are behind and reaching forward to those things which are ahead, I press toward the goal for the prize of the upward call of God in Christ Jesus" (Phil. 3:13–14). If we are going to help in the harvest, we must deny ourselves, take up our cross, and follow Jesus (Matt. 16:24).

Along with blindness and selfishness, some of God's people are guilty of prayerlessness. *Those who sincerely pray for laborers soon become laborers themselves.* Certainly Moses was praying for the Israelites suffering in Egypt, and the Lord called him to deliver them. Nehemiah prayed and wept over the plight of Jerusalem, and God called him to restore the walls and gates of Jerusalem (Neh. 1:4–11). It was in a church prayer meeting that Paul and Barnabas received their call to carry the gospel to the nations (Acts 13:1–3). If our wills are truly surrendered to God, then he may call us to become part of the answer to our own prayers! Many Christians pray the Lord's Prayer faithfully, including "Your kingdom come, Your will be done on earth as it is in heaven." If you really mean that—get ready. God has work for you to do.

Be steadfast, immovable, always abounding in the work of the Lord.

1 Corinthians 15:58

81

39

Jesus answered and said to her, "Martha, Martha, you are worried and troubled about many things. But one thing is needed, and Mary has chosen that good part, which will not be taken away from her."

LUKE 10:41–42

David wrote, "One thing I have desired of the LORD" (Ps. 27:4). Jesus told the rich young ruler, "You still lack one thing" (Luke 18:22). The apostle Paul confessed, "Brethren, I do not count myself to have apprehended; but one thing I do" (Phil. 3:13). Jesus healed a blind beggar who bore witness, saying, "One thing I know: that though I was blind, now I see" (John 9:25). What our Lord said to Martha in our text applies to all of us: "But one thing is needed." In these days, when life can easily be pulled apart and when so many voices tell us what to do, we need to be like Mary and keep our priorities straight. We must make time daily to sit at the feet of Jesus, listen to his Word, and receive truth that is good, needful, and lasting.

If we do this, *we will please the Lord*. There is a time for being a servant like Martha, but it is important that we first take time for worshiping, loving, and learning at the feet of Jesus. This is true preparation for acceptable service. Wherever you find Mary of Bethany in the Scriptures, she is at the feet of Jesus. In our text, she sat at his feet to listen and learn. In John 11:32, she brought her sorrows to his feet, and in John 12:3, she poured out her expensive gift at his feet. In that day, rabbis seldom taught female students, but Jesus was pleased to teach Mary, and he will teach you and me by his Spirit if we come to his feet. Worship and meditation must always precede service, for without Jesus we can do nothing (15:5).

Spending time with Jesus will also *enrich us spiritually*. Martha was worried about food for the body, but Mary's priority was food for the soul. "Do not labor for the food which perishes," Jesus said, "but for the food which endures to everlasting life, which the Son of Man will give you" (6:27). God's word is bread, milk, meat, and honey for the soul (Deut. 8:3; Ps. 119:103; 1 Pet. 2:2–3; Heb. 5:12–14). With her healthy spiritual appetite, Mary was in good company with people like Jeremiah (Jer. 15:16), Job (Job 23:12), and Jesus (Matt. 4:4). Jesus warned us that the cares of this life—like the preparation of meals—can choke the soil of our souls and make it difficult for us to receive the seed of the Word (Luke 8:14). It is essential that we cultivate an appetite for the Word of God and not live on substitutes. Don't settle for secondhand nourishment; let the Spirit teach you directly from Scriptures. That even applies to books like this one, for books are *supplements* to Bible study, not *substitutes* for Bible study and meditation.

Sitting at the feet of Jesus means *you will be criticized*. Satan doesn't mind if your Bible sits on a table or in a drawer, he just doesn't want it to get into your heart and bless you. Martha criticized her sister and her Savior and tried to tell them what to do. Criticism from believers hurts far more than criticism from unbelievers, and we must learn to expect it and not be crippled by it. *Let Jesus defend you just as he defended Mary.* The safest place is at the feet of Jesus.

But the blessing is this: spending time daily with Jesus *will give you lasting influence*. When Mary anointed Jesus, he told her that she would be a blessing to Christians around the world (Matt. 26:13), and she has been! Our lives, our prayers, our worship, and our service can reach around the world and bear fruit for eternity, but we won't know about it until we see Jesus. We must make the choice. Mary made her choice and God blessed her for it.

> I have chosen the way of truth . . .
> I have chosen Your precepts.
> Psalm 119:30, 173

40

> *Do not fear, little flock*, for it is your Father's good
> pleasure to give you the kingdom.

LUKE 12:32

The context of this statement is our Lord's teaching
about worry (Luke 12:22–34). The disciples would be
sent out into a difficult world where evil people and
demanding circumstances would try their faith. Worry can
lead to fear (vv. 4–5), fear can lead to unbelief, and unbelief
always leads to failure. Jesus pointed out that the ravens trust
God for their food and the lilies trust God for their beauty, so
why can't his disciples trust the Father for what they need?
To worry is to live like the Gentiles (v. 30), that is, the unbelieving, idol-worshiping Romans and Greeks of that day.
Rarely does a Christian believer publicly confess the sin of
worry. We prefer to call it "the cross I carry," or "concern,"
or perhaps "trouble." If we would only realize the remarkable relationship we have with the Lord, it would drive away
fear and bring peace.

We are his friends. "And I say to you, My friends, do not
be afraid" (v. 4). Jesus emphasized this relationship in his discourse in the upper room (John 15:13–15). "Greater love has
no one than this, than to lay down one's life for his friends.
You are My friends if you do whatever I command you. No
longer do I call you servants, for a servant does not know what
his master is doing; but I have called you friends, for all things
that I heard from My Father I have made known to you."
The word translated *friends* means "a friend at court." This
was a person close to the king, one who shared his secrets.
"The secret of the LORD is with those who fear Him" (Ps.
25:14), which is why Jesus told his disciples to fear God and
this would conquer every fear (Luke 12:4–7). *Fearing God*

conquers every other fear! "Blessed is the man who fears the LORD . . . his heart is established; he will not be afraid" (Ps. 112:1, 8).

We are his flock. "Do not fear, little flock" (Luke 12:32). The image of the sheep and shepherd is found throughout the Scriptures, referring both to Israel and the church. Sheep are defenseless and not remarkably smart, and they desperately need a shepherd to protect them and provide for them. God's people have always been few in number (Matt. 7:14); we are a "little flock." The world admires big numbers, but God does well even with the small numbers—twelve apostles, 120 believers in Acts 1, Gideon's three hundred soldiers, David's five stones. Contrasted with the accomplishments of the world, the church's ministry may not seem great, *but it will last forever.*

We are his family. The mixed metaphors of sheep, family, and kingdom reflect the eastern background of the Bible, for a sheik was a ruler, a father, and a shepherd. Whoever believes in Jesus Christ becomes the child of the King, and all the King's resources are at our disposal. The Lord doesn't just give us a generous allowance, he gives us the whole kingdom! He "has made us kings and priests to His God and Father" (Rev. 1:6). Why worry and why be afraid when we have available by faith the riches of his grace and the riches of glory (Eph. 1:6; Phil. 4:19)?

Sheep are easily frightened, except when the shepherd is near; and our Shepherd is always near. "Fear not, for I am with you; be not dismayed, for I am your God. I will strengthen you, yes, I will help you, I will uphold you with My righteous right hand" (Isa. 41:10). Don't be afraid of people or circumstances.

> But the very hairs of your head are all numbered. Do not fear therefore; you are of more value than many sparrows.
>
> Luke 12:7

41

And the servant said, "Master, it is done as you commanded, *and still there is room*."

LUKE 14:22

Almighty God, just because he is almighty, needs no support," wrote A. W. Tozer in his excellent book *The Knowledge of the Holy*. God doesn't favor emptiness because he is identified with fullness, except when his Son humbled himself ("emptied himself") to become poor and be born into the human race. But even that event was only the beginning of God's great work of redemption that will climax with a new heaven and a new earth filled with the glory of God. If God is going to fill us for service, he must empty us first.

We see evidence of divine fullness *in God's creation*. According to Genesis 1:2, the earth was characterized by formlessness, darkness, and emptiness until the Lord caused the light to shine; made land, sea, and the heavens; and filled them with life, beauty, and purpose. He bypassed all the other celestial bodies and chose the earth for his own planet. "The earth is the LORD's, and all its fullness, the world and those who dwell therein" (Ps. 24:1). "For the world is Mine, and all its fullness" (50:12). He has filled the world with everything we need for maintaining human life, and his Son came to earth to give us eternal abundant life.

We see God's fullness *in Jesus Christ, the Son of God*, "for it pleased the Father that in Him all the fullness should dwell" (Col. 1:19). Many "religious leaders" have appeared over the centuries, but none of them embodied God as did Jesus. "For in Him all the fullness of Deity dwells in bodily form" (2:9 NASB). There was nothing lacking in the person of Jesus Christ that was essential for life or for the accomplishing of the will of

God. Paradoxically, throughout "the days of his flesh," Jesus Christ was the poorest of the poor and the richest of the rich, and because of his poverty every believer is rich (2 Cor. 8:9).

But the Father wants to see this magnificent fullness energizing *his own spiritual children, the church, the body of Christ.* Jesus is the "head over all things to the church, which is His body, the fullness of Him who fills all in all" (Eph. 1:22–23). Paul was not writing about filling up an auditorium with people but filling the people in the auditorium with the Holy Spirit so they can represent Jesus before a lost and broken world. Our goal is not to become like some well-known Christian. Our goal is to grow "to the measure of the stature of the fullness of Christ" (4:13). It is our fellowship with Christ in the Scriptures, in prayer, in worship, and in service that matures us and transforms us into his image (2 Cor. 3:18). Colossians 2:10 tells us that we are "complete in Him," and John 1:16 that "of His fullness we have all received, and grace for grace." *Read those statements again and believe them.*

At least ten times in the Book of Acts, we read about God's people being "filled with the Spirit," and this was the "secret" of their success. They may not have had much formal education, nor did they have wealth or social status, but they were yielded to the Spirit and obedient to him. They were filled with faith and power (Acts 6:8), filled with rejoicing that they could suffer for Jesus's sake (5:41), and filled with good works that touched the hearts of the people (9:36). This was the beginning of God's glorious fullness in the church, but one day "all the earth shall be filled with the glory of the LORD" (Num. 14:21).

Why not ask God to reveal more of that glory in and through us today?

> For the earth will be filled
> With the knowledge of the glory of the LORD,
> As the waters cover the sea.
>
> Habakkuk 2:14

42

> But the father said to his servants, *"Bring out the best robe* and put it on him, and put a ring on his hand and sandals on his feet."

LUKE 15:22

From Genesis 3:7 to Revelation 22:14, the inspired writers of Scripture have much to say about the spiritual significance of clothing. Washing clothes and changing into clean clothes often symbolizes dramatic changes in the lives of God's people, changes that perhaps some of us need today.

From nakedness to covering. After they had sinned, Adam and Eve tried to cover their shameful nakedness with fig leaves, but the Lord rejected what they had done (Gen. 3:7), just as today he rejects our good works as a way of salvation. Our first parents were acceptable only after the Lord had shed the blood of some innocent animals and clothed Adam and Eve in tunics that he made (3:21). Jesus is the Lamb of God whose blood was shed to take away our sins (John 1:29) and whose righteousness we receive (2 Cor. 5:21).

From defilement to cleansing. Each time I go downstairs into my library, I pass a framed print of Rembrandt's heart-tugging painting *The Return of the Prodigal Son.* (The word *prodigal* means "wasteful.") The boy is on his knees before his father; he is barefoot and dirty, and his clothes are in tatters. He needed new garments, and the "best robe" in the house would belong to his father, who gladly gave it to him. The son was willing to work as a slave, but his father would not hear of it. In his grace and love, the father gave him the garment along with a ring and a pair of shoes. The boy bathed, donned the new clothes, and went to the feast. It was a new beginning! David had a similar experience after confessing his sins (2 Sam. 12:20). When Jacob returned home, he made his whole family wash and change clothes (Gen. 35:1–3).

From an old life to a new life. Joseph took off his prison garments, bathed, and put on clean clothes so he could stand before Pharaoh, and it was the beginning of a new life for him (41:14, 42). He also gave new clothes to his brothers (45:22) as reminders that their old sins were forgiven and gone and the new had come to stay. When, at Mount Sinai, Israel was about to enter into a holy covenant relationship with God, Moses commanded them first to wash their clothes (Exod. 19:10, 14). Jesus raised Lazarus from the dead and commanded that his grave-clothes be removed. Living people don't dress like corpses! Paul used that as an illustration of our taking off the old life and putting on the new (Eph. 4:17–24; Col. 3:1–17). Jesus warned the lukewarm church of Laodicea to put on new spiritual garments and get back to work (Rev. 3:18).

From common clothing to exquisite clothing. The Jewish high priest wore special garments "for glory and for beauty" (Exod. 28:2, 40), and the other priests were also identified by their clothing. After all, they had been set apart by the Lord to serve him alone. If the priests did not dress properly, they were in danger of losing their lives (Exod. 28:43). Brides were also adorned in beautiful garments (Ps. 45:13–15; 132:16; Rev. 21:2). The church is Christ's bride and one day we shall attend that great marriage supper of the Lamb (Rev. 19:7–9). It's important that today we "make ourselves ready" for that grand occasion.

Let's be careful to walk in the Spirit and not defile our garments (3:4). Our Lord says, "Behold, I am coming as a thief. Blessed is he who watches, and keeps his garments, lest he walk naked and they see his shame" (16:15). "Let us be glad and rejoice and give Him glory, for the marriage of the Lamb has come, and His wife has made herself ready" (19:7).

All dressed up and a wonderful place to go—heaven!

Put on the new man which was created according to God, in true righteousness and holiness.

Ephesians 4:24

43

> Then He spoke a parable to them, that *men always ought to pray* and not lose heart.
>
> LUKE 18:1

Prayer is both the thermometer and the thermostat of the Christian life. It reveals our "spiritual temperature" and also helps to regulate it. If we are neglecting prayer or if we are praying listlessly, then we are "cold" (Matt. 24:12). If we are "up and down" in an undisciplined prayer life, we are "lukewarm," neither hot nor cold (Rev. 3:15–16). If we are walking with the Lord, meditating on the Word and yielded to him, our hearts will "burn within us" and energize us (Luke 24:32). Being honest in answering these questions in a brief inventory can help us improve our prayer ministry.

Have we lost the wonder of prayer? Do we remember how excited we were to be privileged to visit the throne of grace and talk to our heavenly Father? I came to Christ a few days short of my sixteenth birthday, and the very next week I attended prayer meeting. I also began to attend a home fellowship devoted to Bible study and prayer. I was not the pastor of the church nor was I a mature believer, *yet my heavenly Father would listen to me.* When we lose the wonder of prayer, our praying becomes routine, burdensome, and selfish. Yes, prayer is an obligation—note the word "ought" in our text—but it must be obeyed with wonder in our hearts.

Are we delighted with the worship involved in prayer? When I was a child, I often heard my mother phone the local grocery store and read her "want list." An hour or so later, the delivery boy would be at our door carrying bags of groceries. But that isn't what prayer is about! God knows our needs before we mention them, *and we don't always know our needs.* We ask for a better job when what we really need is a better attitude in our present job. When we worship the Lord and "get lost" in his greatness, we get a better perspective on life and on God's promises in the Scriptures. There are crisis experiences in life (like Peter sinking into the sea) when all we can do is cry out for help, but most of the time we can "take time to behold him" and worship our great God. Moses spent forty days and nights on the mountain with Jehovah, and we have trouble investing forty minutes in his glorious presence.

Have we learned what it means to wrestle in prayer? Sometimes our prayer experience is like that of a child in a parent's lap, simply talking and listening and loving. But sometimes it's like Jacob wrestling with the Lord, asking for protection for himself and his family (Gen. 32:22–32), or like God's servant Epaphras, "laboring fervently" in prayer for the church in Colossae (Col. 4:12). The word translated *laboring* means "to agonize, to struggle." It pictures an athlete giving his or her best at the Greek Olympics. We don't wrestle with God to try to change his will but to be honest with him in expressing our true feelings. In true prayer, there is no place for pretending, for God knows our hearts.

Do we recognize the tragedy of fainting? If we don't pray, we will faint; it's as simple as that. It may take time, but eventually we will run out of our own energy and the crisis will occur, as it did with King Saul, Jonah, and Peter. It is those who "wait upon the Lord" who "renew their strength" and can keep running, walking, and flying when circumstances demand it (Isa. 40:31). The most successful spiritual leaders found in Scripture and in church history were people who took their weaknesses to the Lord in prayer and let him transform them into overcoming power (2 Cor. 12:7–10). Some of the records are in Hebrews 11. Have you read it lately?

And He said to me, "My grace is sufficient for you, for My strength is made perfect in weakness."

2 Corinthians 12:9

44

In the beginning was the Word, and the Word was with God, *and the Word was God.*

JOHN 1:1

The voice of the Lord spoken through the prophets was silent during the four centuries between Malachi and John the Baptist. Then John the Baptist came as "a voice crying in the wilderness" (John 1:23), preparing the way for Jesus who is the Word (Rev. 19:13). He is also the "alpha and omega," the first and last "letters" of the Greek alphabet. In this prologue to John's Gospel (1:1–18), we are introduced to Jesus Christ in three dramatic statements.

Jesus always was. He existed before creation and together with the Father and the Spirit brought everything into being (v. 3). "For by Him all things were created that are in heaven and that are on earth. . . . All things were created through Him and for Him" (Col. 1:16). Jesus did not come into existence when he was conceived by the Spirit in Mary's womb, because he had existed before creation itself. How did the Trinity bring creation into being? By the Word! In the first two chapters of Genesis, you find God speaking twelve times and bringing into existence the heavens and the earth and all that is in them. "By the word of the LORD the heavens were made . . . for He spoke, and it was done; He commanded, and it stood fast" (Ps. 33:6, 9). Why is Jesus called "the Word"? Just as our words reveal our heart, mind, and character, so Jesus the Word reveals to us the heart, mind, and character of God. Jesus said, "He who has seen Me has seen the Father" (John 14:9). John emphasizes that Jesus is eternal God and the only Savior of sinners (John 20:31). Anyone who denies this is not a Christian (1 John 4:1–6).

Jesus always was with the Father. The phrase "with God" literally means "face to face with God," and it speaks of intimacy. John 1:18 tells us that the Son is "in the bosom of the Father." Every believer is in the Father and the Son through the indwelling of the Holy Spirit (14:20). All the time Jesus was here on earth, he was in fellowship with the Father. Jesus lived because of the Father (6:37), and together they did the work of the ministry (5:17; 10:37). Jesus did his Father's will (5:30) and spoke the words given to him by the Father (15:15). Our Lord sought only to honor his Father (8:49), and for that reason, the Father honored the Son (v. 54). The only time the Father forsook the Son was when Jesus on the cross was made sin for us (2 Cor. 5:21) and cried, "My God, My God, why have You forsaken Me?" (Matt. 27:46; see Ps. 22:1).

Jesus was always God and always will be. Near the end of the first century, when John wrote his Gospel and epistles, false teachers were teaching that Jesus was not the Son of God. John wrote his Gospel so that his readers might "believe that Jesus is the Christ, the Son of God" and have life in his name (John 20:31). Jesus himself testifies that he is the Son of God (3:18; 5:25; 9:35; 11:4). His enemies even raised this issue at his trial (19:7). Throughout his book, John quotes witnesses who testified that Jesus is God come in human flesh: John the Baptist (1:29–34), Nathanael (v. 49), Peter (6:69), the blind man Jesus cured (9:35–38), Martha (11:27), Thomas (20:28), and the apostle John himself (v. 31). It has always been the testimony of the true church that Jesus is the only begotten Son of God. The phrase "only begotten" (1:14, 18) simply means "unique, one of a kind." There has never been, nor is there now, anyone on earth or in heaven who is exactly like Jesus, for he is unique. But one day "we shall be like Him, for we shall see Him as He is" (1 John 3:2).

Hallelujah, what a Savior!

> These are written that you may believe that Jesus is the Christ, the Son of God, and that believing you may have life in His name.
>
> John 20:31

45

Then Jesus turned, and seeing them following, said to them, "What do you seek?" They said to Him, "Rabbi" (which is to say, when translated, *Teacher*), *"where are You staying?"*

JOHN 1:38

Great crowds gathered to hear John the Baptist, and many believed and were baptized, among them John and Andrew. The quiet drama that played out on the day described in John 1:35–42 was actually part of God's plan for redeeming a lost world.

Act 1—following the Lamb. It was John the Baptist's purpose to point people to Jesus and not to gather permanent disciples around himself. "He must increase," John said, "but I must decrease" (John 3:30). Among the men in John's congregation were John and Andrew, two partners in a fishing business in Capernaum. When John the Baptist pointed to Jesus and cried out, "Behold the Lamb of God!" the two men left the crowd and followed Jesus (vv. 36–37). Trusting Jesus is the beginning of the Christian life, but only the beginning.

Act 2—facing a decision. Knowing that the two men were following him, Jesus turned and asked them, "What do you seek?" (v. 38). Why did people follow Jesus when he was ministering here on earth? Some wanted to be entertained by his miracles, while others sincerely sought his teaching. Some were only members of the crowd, while others stepped out of the crowd and identified themselves personally with the Savior. Jesus saves and transforms people one at a time, not *en masse*. We must examine our hearts to determine if our motives are right as we seek to follow the Lord and serve him. Right actions can be defiled by wrong motives.

Act 3—obeying a command. Perhaps the two men did not really know what they were seeking, and that's why they replied with a question of their own, "Teacher, where are you staying?" (v. 38). A young Jewish student asked his rabbi, "Why is it whenever I ask you a question, you always answer with another question?" The rabbi replied, "And why shouldn't I?" It's likely that Andrew and John wanted to accommodate themselves to our Lord's schedule and therefore offered to visit him later, so they asked where he lived. But Jesus wanted to speak with them *now.* "Behold, now is the accepted time; behold, now is the day of salvation" (2 Cor. 6:2). "Come" is a familiar word from the lips of Jesus, a gracious invitation from his heart. "Come and see" leads to "Come and drink" (John 7:37–39), and "Come and eat" (21:12). Where does Jesus dwell? Not in temples or shrines made by human hands (Acts 7:48–50), but "in the high and holy place, with him who has a contrite and humble spirit, to revive the spirit of the humble, and to revive the heart of the contrite ones" (Isa. 57:15). John and Andrew were humble fishermen who had no idea what the Lord would do for them and through them in the years to come. "God resists the proud, but gives grace to the humble" (1 Pet. 5:5).

Act 4—sharing the good news. Listening to Jesus convinced the two men that Jesus was indeed the promised Messiah, and they had to tell others. Andrew found his brother Simon and brought him to Jesus, and we have every reason to believe that John found his brother James as well. The four men returned to their fishing business until that day when Jesus called them to become fishers of men (Luke 5:1–11).

Jesus has stayed in many places, but the one place he enjoys the most is the contrite and humble heart of his obedient disciples who are proclaiming to the world, "Behold the Lamb of God!"

Behold, I stand at the door and knock.

Revelation 3:20

95

46

Do not marvel that I said to you, *"You must be born again."*

JOHN 3:7

The phrase "born again" has been borrowed from the Bible and put into the secular world to replace "remodel" or "makeover." What was once "used furniture" is now "born again furniture." This has no connection with personal regeneration, receiving new life and a new nature from God through faith in Jesus Christ. These new definitions might be in your dictionary or thesaurus, but if you discussed them with Nicodemus, he would tell you that there is a world of difference between remodeled furniture and a regenerated sinner who has been transformed into a child of God. Nicodemus experienced it!

He went from death to birth. When spiritually dead sinners trust Jesus Christ, they move from death to life. "And you He made alive, who were dead in trespasses and sins" (Eph. 2:1). Nicodemus was shocked when Jesus said his old birth was unacceptable to God and he needed a new birth. He was born a Jew! Could there be any higher birth than that? The Jews were God's chosen people and his treasure. God delivered them from bondage and gave them their own land. He gave them the Scriptures and fought their battles, and through Israel brought Jesus Christ into the world to die for sinners. Why would a religious man like Nicodemus ("the teacher of Israel," John 3:10) have to start all over again? Because God rejects our first birth and accepts only a second birth through faith in Christ. Not only did Nicodemus need to be born again, but so did the entire Jewish council, the Sanhedrin, to which he belonged. In the Greek text of John 3:7, the first "you" is singular and refers to Nicodemus, but the second "you" is plural and refers to the Jewish religious leaders in the council. They all needed to be born again.

He went from tradition to truth. Like the men in the Jewish council and many religious people today, Nicodemus studied the sacred books and the traditions of the elders; but he had failed to learn that "the just shall live by his faith" (Hab. 2:4; *see* Rom 1:17; Gal. 3:11; Heb. 10:38). We are not saved by good character or good religious works but by faith in Jesus Christ and him alone. In John 7:45–52, you find Nicodemus defending Jesus in a council meeting, and the officers said to him, "Search and look, for no prophet has arisen out of Galilee" (v. 52). Nicodemus and his friend Joseph of Arimathea, another council member, did just that. They studied the prophets and discovered that Jesus of Nazareth was indeed the Son of God, the Messiah. They learned that the Messiah would be crucified on Passover, and they prepared Joseph's tomb near Calvary to receive his dead body. I believe they were in that tomb with the spices and linen wrappings while Jesus was on the cross. Joseph got permission to bury our Lord's body. Because they touched a corpse, Joseph and Nicodemus could not eat the Passover lamb—but they had trusted the Lamb of God, so it made no difference!

He went from darkness to light. Every baby born into this world moves from the darkness of the womb into the light of the world, and so does the newly born child of God. Jesus is the Light of the world (8:12). He had already talked to Nicodemus about this (3:19–21). When we first meet Nicodemus, he is in the dark (vv. 1–2); but the last time we see him in Scripture, it is midafternoon and he is openly giving witness of his faith in Christ (19:38–42). "He who does the truth comes to the light," said Jesus (3:21).

Blessed are those who have experienced these three changes!

> He who follows Me shall not walk in darkness, but have the light of life.
>
> John 8:12

47

You worship what you do not know; we know
what we worship, for *salvation is from the Jews.*

JOHN 4:22

That Jesus spoke to this woman doesn't surprise you
and me, but it must have shocked her, because rabbis
did not speak to women in public. No doubt she asked
herself, *What is this man up to?* But Jesus knew more about
her than she knew about herself (John 2:24–25).

He knew she was trapped in the wrong lifestyle. When
Jesus asked about her husband, the truth came out. She had
been married to five different husbands, and the man she
was now living with was not her husband. She was thirst-
ing for life but was drinking at the wrong well. She should
have learned her lesson after the first or second divorce, but
individual acts of sin slowly become a yoke of bondage that
controls us (Lam. 1:14). Addicts assure themselves, "We can
stop when we please," but then they discover they are trapped.
The Japanese have a saying: "First the man takes a drink,
then the drink takes a drink, then the drink takes the man."

He knew she was raised in the wrong religion. I was waiting for a plane in the Kansas City airport when a young man
carrying a colorful book sat down next to me. "I'd like to
introduce you to the savior of the world," he said. "Where
does he come from?" I asked. He replied, "He's Korean." I
reached into my briefcase and took out my Bible. "According
to this book, the Savior of the world is Jewish." He was up
and gone before I could say another word. Our text comes
from the lips of Jesus himself. The Jews are God's chosen
people (Deut. 7:6) who taught the world about the true and
living God and who gave the world the Scriptures and the
Savior of the world, Jesus Christ. Jesus did not believe that

one religion is as good as another. The life we have in Jesus Christ is available nowhere else. There are true worshipers and false worshipers (John 4:22–23), and only the true worshipers are going to heaven (14:6).

How do you help people like this? You lovingly lead them into the truth about Jesus and invite them to put their faith in him. Jesus did this and see what happened!

She made the right decision. First she called Jesus "a Jew" (4:9), then a prophet (v. 19), and then the Messiah (vv. 25, 29); the people of the city who trusted Christ through her witness called him "the Savior of the world" (v. 42). How they handled the false Samaritan religion from then on, we don't know, but no doubt they won many more to the Savior.

She set the right example. Forgiven of her sins, she became an effective witness of the Lord Jesus Christ. The people of the city may have heard John the Baptist preach (John 3:23; 4:25), and this helped prepare their hearts for Christ's message; later Philip would minister there, and also Peter and John (Acts 8:4–25). When a pastor shares the gospel, people look upon him as a paid salesman; but when the people of the church witness, they are seen as satisfied customers! The Lord transformed this much-married woman into a powerful witness.

There was deep conflict between the Jews and the Samaritans (John 4:9). I wonder if these new Christians reminded the rest of the city that "salvation is of the Jews"? Jesus broke down the wall that stood between the Jews and the Gentiles so that all who believe in Jesus are members of one body and living stones in one temple (Eph. 2:11–22). There is no place in the church for segregation, for we are all one in Christ (Gal. 3:26–29).

Beloved, let us love one another, for love is of God; and everyone who loves is born of God and knows God.

1 John 4:7

48

Jesus answered them, "*My Father has been working* until now, and I have been working."

JOHN 5:17

Jesus healed a man on the Sabbath day and was severely criticized by his legalistic enemies, who even wanted to kill him for breaking their law (John 5:16). The man he healed had been afflicted for thirty-eight years, and Jesus could have avoided trouble by waiting just one more day, but he wanted to make a point. In healing the man, he was only doing what his Father was also doing—graciously working on behalf of the people. Christ's reply only angered the Pharisees more, because Jesus was claiming to be equal with God. He and the Father were working together!

God is at work in the world. He finished creation and turned planet Earth over to Adam and his descendants (Ps. 8), but God is still in charge. He built into the universe laws that govern its operation, and he is privileged to interrupt those laws if it pleases him. In his insightful book *The Miracles of Jesus*, George MacDonald points out that, in Christ's miracles, Jesus did *instantly* what the Father is always doing *gradually*. Jesus multiplied bread instantly, but the Father gives us harvests year after year so we can bake bread. Day after day, the Father helps sick and injured people to get well, but Jesus healed them instantly. In vineyards and vats, the Father is turning water into wine, but Jesus did it instantly. The Father uses natural laws to bring babies into the world, but the Son instantly gives new birth spiritually to those who trust him. In his wonderful providence, God works on behalf of his creation, including us. Were it not so, we could never claim Romans 8:28. Yet people ignore what the Father is doing, oppose it, and even seek to destroy it. This is our

Father's world, and we must be grateful to him for it and be good stewards of his precious gifts.

Satan the adversary is also at work in the world. "For the mystery of lawlessness is already at work," Paul wrote (2 Thess. 2:7). The word *mystery* does not refer to something ghostly or bizarre. In the New Testament, a mystery is a divine secret hidden in God's plan and understood only with God's help. The "mystery of lawlessness" refers to the Satanic plan now in operation to bring the false Christ into the world at the close of the age. The word *antichrist* means not only "against Christ" but also "instead of Christ." Satan is a counterfeiter (2 Cor. 11:13–15), and sinners prefer his fake merchandise to the true riches they can have in Jesus. Satan is at work—so what should we do?

God's people should be at work in the world. "I must work the works of Him who sent me while it is day; the night is coming when no one can work" (John 9:4). We as Christ's disciples must be like him and be about the Father's business (Luke 2:49). This not only refers to making a living but also to making a life that will influence others to trust Jesus. "My food," Jesus said, "is to do the will of Him who sent Me, and to finish His work" (John 4:34). Doing the will of God is not punishment; it is nourishment. It makes people grow and glow so they can help others trust the Savior. Seven times in Revelation 2–3, our Lord says to churches, "I know your works." One day our works will be examined at the judgment seat of Christ (Rom. 14:10–12) and we will be rewarded according to what we have done for Jesus, how we did it, and why we did it (1 Cor. 4:1–5). If the Holy Spirit is working in us and through us, we have nothing to fear (Phil. 1:6; Acts 1:8). Jesus "went about doing good" (Acts 10:38), and his is the example we should follow.

> He who has begun a good work in you will complete it until the day of Jesus Christ.
>
> Philippians 1:6

49

There is a lad here who has five barley loaves and two small fish, but what are they among so many?

When we find ourselves in a difficult situation, we must remember John 6:6, "He Himself knew what He would do." Jesus always has a plan and will share it with us if we let him. Philip thought the problem would be solved if they had more money (v. 7), but Jesus had a better plan and Andrew helped him expedite it. "There is a lad here" solved the problem. The boy was part of the answer and not part of the problem, and so may we be if we follow his example. Let's take inventory.

Am I willing to act alone? Children are great imitators, but there is no evidence that anybody else in the crowd brought out a lunch. When Andrew asked him to share his lunch with Jesus, the boy said he would. Never underestimate the importance of one person or what that person may have in his or her hand. During my years of pastoral ministry, I have asked people to assist in projects, and too often have heard the same question: "Who else is helping?" Are we willing to stand alone, give alone, and work alone? But we are not alone! We are working with the Master, and "we are God's fellow workers" (1 Cor. 3:9). Is there any greater honor?

Am I willing to give Jesus my all? In that day, the average poor person's lunch would consist of barley cakes and fish, not wheat bread and roast beef. This was all that the boy had, and yet he was willing to give it all to Jesus. God measures our gifts not by the portion but by the proportion. After we have given our gift, how much is left over? The poor widow who gave two mites (less than one penny) gave more that day than all the rich people who preceded her, because she gave all that she had (Mark 12:41–44). If we obey Romans 12:1–2 and lay our all on the altar, we will have no problem giving generously to Christ and sacrificing for others. Jesus gave his all for us and he wants us to give our all to him, not that he might rob us but that he might enrich us and bless us. "Give, and it will be given to you. A good measure, pressed down, shaken together and running over, will be poured into your lap" (Luke 6:38 TNIV).

Am I willing to be anonymous? We know next to nothing about this lad. He joins the ranks of the large number of unnamed people who played important parts in the plan of God. What was the name of Paul's nephew whose warning saved Paul's life (Acts 23:11–22)? Who was the girl who told Naaman about the prophet in Samaria (2 Kings 5), or the woman at the well who introduced the townspeople to Jesus (John 4)? I sometimes receive requests for money for projects, promising to put my name on a plaque if I give generously. And if I really give generously, they will name a room in a new building after me. Is that why we give? "But when you do a charitable deed," Jesus said, "do not let your left hand know what your right hand is doing" (Matt. 6:3). Why? Because if we did, we would proudly pat ourselves on the back!

Am I willing for Jesus to get all the glory? When the crowd had finished the meal, and all the fragments had been gathered, the people didn't applaud the lad who donated the food. No, they wanted to make Jesus king (John 6:15). Their motive was wrong, of course, but at least their focus was on Christ. When we pray for the Holy Spirit to fill and use us, do we remember that the ministry of the Spirit is to glorify Jesus? "He will glorify Me," said Jesus (16:14). If what we do points only to ourselves, the Spirit cannot bless. There is nothing the Father cannot do for those who want Jesus to get the glory and who don't care who gets the credit.

> I beseech you therefore, brethren, by the mercies of God, that you present your bodies a living sacrifice, holy, acceptable to God, which is your reasonable service.
>
> Romans 12:1

50

> Then Jesus said to them, "My time has not yet come, but *your time is always ready.*"

JOHN 7:6

Almost everybody is busy and wants to get more done in less time. The problem is not that we have time on our hands but that we need to get our hands on our time. The brief discussion about *time* that Jesus had with his unbelieving half-brothers (John 7:1–9) helps us better understand the spiritual significance of time and how Christians can make time count.

The arrogance of the world. The law of Moses required that every Jewish male attend three annual feasts in Jerusalem: Passover, the Feast of Weeks, and the Feast of Tabernacles (Deut. 16:16). The advice of our Lord's unbelieving half-brothers certainly reveals the outlook of the unsaved world: "Go early to the feast! Do great things! Capture their attention! Make yourself known!" Jesus was the servant of God and they wanted him to become a celebrity applauded by men. But Jesus rejected their advice because he took his orders from the Father. He was not interested in getting glory for himself; he wanted only to glorify the Father (John 7:18). Satan had already made that offer to Jesus and he had turned it down (Matt. 4:8–11). It's sad when God's servants obey the voices of the world and ultimately become famous failures. *The unsaved world can do what they will at any time because they aren't on God's schedule.* They have no interest in knowing or doing the will of God. But every step Jesus took brought him closer to the cross (Luke 9:51) and he was not interested in detours.

The obedience of the Savior. John's Gospel emphasizes the fact that Jesus was living on a divine timetable. The first chapter gives a day-by-day account of his activities as he began his ministry, and in subsequent chapters we find him often referring to his "hour." He told his mother, "My hour has not yet come" (2:4), and in our text he tells his half-brothers, "My time has not yet come" (*see* 8:20, 12:23, 27; 13:1; 17:1). Jesus knew that the religious leaders wanted to kill him (7:1, 11) and that this would eventually happen during his last Passover. He was protected by the Father until that time arrived. So long as they do God's will, God's people are immortal until their work is done, and then they will be called home. Early each morning, Jesus arose and went to a secluded place where he communed with the Father (Mark 1:35; Isa. 50:4), an example each of us should follow. If we pray "Your will be done," then we had better know what that will is and be ready to obey it.

The confidence of the believer. Jesus may have had Psalm 31:15 in mind when he spoke to his half-brothers: "My times are in Your hand." The children of God must exercise faith and patience if they are to receive what the Lord has promised (Heb. 6:12). It has well been said that God's delays are not God's denials. God has to prepare us for what he has prepared for us, and that takes time. Joseph tried to get out of prison sooner, but the plan didn't work because the time was not right. David had been anointed king of Israel, but he had to wait over seven years after Saul died before all twelve tribes crowned him.

Unsaved people have no divine schedule to fulfill and, as Jesus said, their time "is always ready," but believers have a responsibility to know and do God's will in God's time. Even a Christian's death is not an unplanned accident but a part of the Father's loving plan. "Precious in the sight of the LORD is the death of His saints" (Ps. 116:15). I heard about a believer who said, "Well, we will just have to pray for good luck." But we don't live by chance or by luck! We live by the plan and providence of God. He is Jehovah Jireh, "The-LORD-Will-Provide" (Gen. 22:14). And he will!

My times are in Your hand.

Psalm 31:15

51

Therefore if the Son makes you free, *you shall be free indeed.*

To some, freedom means the opportunity to do what they want to do. To most it means not to do what they do not want to do." So wrote British novelist and essayist George Orwell, but I question his definition. To me, true freedom is life controlled by truth and motivated by love, to the glory of God. Dead people have no freedom, nor do people who believe lies or act out of meanness and selfishness. Physical freedom is useless if we don't have spiritual freedom, for it is only in spiritual freedom that we have divine life, truth, and love.

Life comes from conception and birth. The people our Lord addressed in this chapter boasted that they were free and that their nation always had been free. This was, of course, an outright lie. The book of Judges tells us that Israel had been enslaved by seven nations. Later history shows that Assyria enslaved the northern kingdom and Babylon the southern kingdom, and at that very hour, the Jews were enslaved by Rome! The worst slavery is not political or physical but ethical and moral, the kind of slavery people experience because they have never had a spiritual rebirth by trusting Jesus Christ. "Most assuredly, I say to you," Jesus said, "whoever commits [repeatedly practices] sin is a slave of sin" (John 8:34). Only the Son, Jesus Christ, can set us free from spiritual death and slavery and give us freedom and eternal life. Dead people are not free, and all who have never trusted Christ are "dead in trespasses and sins" (Eph. 2:1). Liberty begins with life, and spiritual life comes only by faith in Jesus Christ.

Spiritual conception and birth occur when we believe God's truth. We are born again through the Spirit of God (John

106

3:1–8) using the Word of God (1 Pet. 1:23) to generate our faith in the Son of God. We cannot fully explain the new birth because it is a miracle, but we can still experience it and enjoy it. By faith we are born into God's family and become "partakers of the divine nature" (2 Pet. 1:2–4), new creations in Christ (2 Cor. 5:17). There is no other way to receive the life of God except by believing the truth of God and being born again. The Son of God is truth (John 14:6), the Word of God is truth (17:17), and the Spirit of God is truth (1 John 5:6), and they work together to convict us and then give us eternal life. The people Jesus was speaking to in John 8 opposed God's truth (v. 40) and were unwilling to receive it (v. 43). "And you shall know the truth, and the truth shall make you free" (v. 32).

The new birth replaces selfishness with love. Jesus said to his rebellious listeners, "If God were your Father, you would love Me, for I proceeded forth and came from God" (v. 42). A heart filled with love for God and God's people is one of the marks of the new birth (Rom. 5:1–5; 1 John 3:13–17), for "the fruit of the Spirit is love" (Gal. 5:22). Freedom is life controlled by truth and motivated by love, and truth and love must go together. We must speak the truth in love (Eph. 4:15) and remember that love does not rejoice in iniquity but rejoices in the truth (1 Cor. 13:6). If we are motivated by love, we will want to live and work for God's glory alone. Christian love "does not parade itself, is not puffed up" (v. 4).

The apostle Peter warns us against a false freedom that ultimately leads to the worst kind of bondage (2 Pet. 2:18–22). These professed Christians never received the divine new nature and became sheep but instead remained dogs and hogs. The dog may empty its stomach and feel better and the hog may be washed and look better, but they are still in bondage to the old nature. They knew the way of salvation but never walked on it. Beware of a false freedom!

Unless one is born again, he cannot see the kingdom of God.

John 3:3

52

I am the good shepherd. The good shepherd gives
His life for the sheep.

A flock of sheep is one of the most familiar metaphors in Scripture for the people of God. The Old
Testament believer prayed, "Give ear, O Shepherd
of Israel, You who lead Joseph like a flock" (Ps. 80:1); and
the new covenant Christian knows Jesus as the good shepherd and the local church as his flock (Acts 20:28–29). The
leader of a local flock is called "pastor" (Eph. 4:11), which
comes from a Latin word meaning "to feed, to shepherd."
In the nation of Israel, the civil leaders were also known as
shepherds because they were caring for God's flock. Unfortunately, not all of Israel's shepherds were faithful to the Lord
or to his sheep, and the prophets had to warn them and the
Lord had to judge them (Ezek. 34; Jer. 23:1–4; Isa. 56:9–12).
They *drove* the sheep instead of *leading* them and robbed
them instead of feeding and caring for them. Jesus warned
the people against thieves and robbers and the hirelings, the
selfish, grasping, false shepherds who were more interested
in money and power than in ministry and compassion.

Jesus is our *good* shepherd, a word that in the Greek means
"choice, best, blameless, praiseworthy, and beautiful." Let's
give thanks for all he means to us and does for us!

He died for us. "The good shepherd gives His life for the
sheep" (John 10:11). "I lay down My life for the sheep" (v. 15).
"I lay down My life that I may take it again" (v. 17). In the
Old Testament, the sheep died on the altar for the shepherd,
but under the new covenant, the Shepherd died on the cross
for his sheep! He knows us personally and intimately and he
calls us by name (v. 3). He gives us eternal life and abundant

life (vv. 10, 28). How could we question his love when he yielded his life on the cross for us?

He lives for us. "Now may the God of peace who brought up our Lord Jesus from the dead, that great Shepherd of the sheep . . . make you complete in every good work to do His will, working in you what is well pleasing in His sight, through Jesus Christ, to whom be glory forever and ever" (Heb. 13:20–21). Jesus the High Priest intercedes for us in heaven, and we have access to the mercy seat at all times (4:14–16). He goes before us, and not only leads the way but prepares the way, and we have nothing to fear. He lives and he serves.

He speaks to us and leads us. The word *voice* is used five times in John 10 (vv. 3–5, 16, 27) and refers to the Spirit speaking to us by the Scriptures. One sure mark of genuine believers is their appetite for the Word of God and their desire to understand and obey it. A true Christian can detect the voice of a hireling, a thief, or a false prophet and wants nothing to do with them. Jesus wants to lead us into the rich green pastures of his Word and nourish us in spiritual truth. "My sheep hear My voice, and I know them, and they follow Me" (v. 27). To those not in his flock, he will one day say, "I never knew you" (Matt. 7:21–23).

He will come for us. Peter wrote to the pastors and their flocks that "when the Chief Shepherd appears, you will receive the crown of glory that does not fade away" (1 Pet. 5:4). The shepherd's work is not easy but it will be amply rewarded, and sheep who have made the shepherd's work even more difficult will be dealt with by the Lord (Heb. 13:17).

The arrogant false shepherds reviled the beggar and excommunicated him from the synagogue, but the good shepherd found him and added him to his flock (John 9:28–29, 34–41). The leaders had beheld a miracle yet were blind to their own sins and to the Son of God. Are we also blind?

"You are My flock, the flock of My pasture; you are men, and I am your God," says the Lord GOD.

Ezekiel 34:31

53

Martha said to Jesus, "Lord, *if You had been here*, my brother would not have died."

JOHN 11:21

Disappointment, sickness, death, and sorrow are woven into the fabric of our lives, and when they come, we must not be surprised. We must face them honestly and deal with them courageously by faith. Understanding three little words in John 11 can help us.

If *is the word that hurts*. Jesus and his disciples were staying at Bethabara (John 10:40; *see* 1:28), about twenty miles from Bethany; and it took the sisters' messenger at least a day to get there. But before that day ended, Lazarus died (11:39) and Jesus knew it; *yet he remained where he was!* John assures us that "Jesus loved Martha and her sister and Lazarus" (v. 5). But if he loved them, why didn't he hurry to Bethany and heal Lazarus, or just speak the word and heal from a distance? But God's delays are not God's denials, and Jesus had something better planned for the two sisters: Lazarus would glorify God (v. 40). Jesus waited two days and then went to Bethany. Both Martha and Mary (v. 32) used this painful word *if* when they met Jesus, and you and I have used it too. "*If* we had taken a different route." "*If* I had remembered the appointment." "*If* she had never left home." The word *if* hurts because it's a word of unbelief, and unbelief only makes matters worse. *When we say* if *to the Lord, we are saying that he doesn't know what he is doing and that we have a better plan*. We are looking back instead of looking up. We should say "Lord" but forget about the *if*. Jesus *is* here with us (Matt. 28:20).

Lord *is the word that heals*. It is used eight times in John 11, six times by the sisters. To call Jesus *Lord* is to affirm that he is the Son of God and the Master of everything in our lives, but to call him *Lord* and question his will is not evidence of strong faith. Jesus had sent his message to the sisters, saying, "This sickness is not unto death, but for the glory of God, that the Son of God may be glorified through it" (John 11:4). Whenever we are disappointed with the will of God, it's time to affirm our faith in his wisdom and his love. In spite of what happens and no matter how much we hurt, God loves us, and you can put your own name in verses 3, 5, and 36. Never forget that the will of God comes from the loving heart of God (Ps. 33:11), and though the Lord may hurt us, he will never harm us. He is the Lord of life and death (John 11:25–26) and he will work out everything for our good and his glory. It's easy to say the word *Lord* with our lips and yet have reservations in our heart, and this grieves the Lord. Another word must come before *Lord*.

Yes *is the word that heartens.* Martha's "Yes, Lord, I believe" (v. 27) was the turning point in the whole occasion. When we say *yes* to the Lord, and not, "Not so, Lord," as Peter did (Acts 10:14), we win the smile of his approval and the grace we need to trust him, obey him, and allow him to work. Our *yes* of faith transforms misery into miracle. When at the grave, Martha began to resist (vv. 39–40) until Jesus reassured her, and she agreed to open the grave. Jesus spoke the word and God's power gave Lazarus life and carried him to the door of the tomb (his feet were bound). God was glorified, not only in the resurrection of Lazarus but also in the faith of the spectators who trusted Jesus (v. 45; *see* 12:17–19).

The next time the situation is difficult, let's say *yes* to the Lord and ask that he be glorified. He will take care of the rest and our hearts will be at peace.

> For all the promises of God in Him are Yes, and in Him Amen, to the glory of God through us.
>
> 2 Corinthians 1:20

54

Fear not, daughter of Zion; *behold, your King is coming*, sitting on a donkey's colt.

JOHN 12:15

A day arrived when the people of Israel simply had to have a king. They told Samuel, their godly prophet and judge, to ask the Lord for a king, and he gave them Saul, son of Kish (1 Sam. 8), who turned out to be a dismal failure and almost ruined the nation. Beware of the burdens of answers to selfish prayers. The people had not rejected Samuel, they had rejected the Lord (v. 7). They wanted to be like the other nations (v. 20) when the Lord had made them *different* from the other nations and wanted them to stay that way (Num. 26:9). How like churches today that become more like the world, hoping that this compromise will reach the lost. The day came when Israel's King, Jesus Christ, was among them, and on what we call Palm Sunday he rode like a king into Jerusalem. The people welcomed him enthusiastically, even though the Passover visitors didn't even know who he was. It's one thing to be in a crowd, seeming to follow Jesus, and quite something else to acknowledge him with an obedient will and a loving heart. A few days later, another crowd was shouting, "Crucify Him! Crucify Him! We have no king but Caesar" (John 19:15). "You shall not follow a crowd to do evil" (Exod. 23:2).

At Christ's birth, the magi traveled a long distance to acknowledge Jesus as King and to present him with valuable gifts (Matt. 2:1–12). They were Gentiles, but they worshiped the King of the Jews, for they knew he was the Savior of the world. God used a star to guide them to his Son. That isn't likely to happen today, but God does still use various means to bring people to Jesus—a sermon, a gospel tract, a song, a seeming tragedy, the witness of a believer, the kind deed of a Christian friend. Whenever we bear witness to Jesus, let's remember that he is King of Kings and we need not be ashamed.

Throughout his ministry, Jesus made it clear that he was King. He ruled over the wind and the waves, and when he spoke, they obeyed. The water of the Sea of Galilee held him up as if it were concrete (Matt. 14:22–33). The demons recognized him and trembled, and he sent them to the pit. The dominion that God gave Adam and Eve was lost because of their disobedience, but when Jesus came to earth, he was in command of weather, animals, trees, fish, and birds. All of nature obeyed him while people made in God's image rejected him. He was King even when he was nailed to a cross! It was customary to put an announcement over the head of the victim declaring his offense, and Pilate wrote about Jesus, "JESUS OF NAZARETH, KING OF THE JEWS" (John 19:19). For six hours, Jesus reigned from the cross, and everything that happened fulfilled the prophecies and plans of God.

Today, Jesus is enthroned in heaven, seated at the Father's right hand, far above every authority, including Satan and his demonic army, and Jesus alone is the head of the church (Eph. 1:20–23). He is "King of glory" (Ps. 24:7–10), and one day we shall share that glory (John 17:24). When Jesus rode into Jerusalem, he fulfilled the prophecy of Zechariah 9:9; but when he comes for his people, he will keep the promise he has made to his church, "I will come again" (John 14:1–6). He will reign as "King of kings" (Rev. 19:16) and King of the whole world (Zech. 14:9). We shall reign with him and serve him in ways for which our faithful ministries on earth have prepared us (Matt. 25:14–30).

Pray much! Work faithfully! Keep clean! Look up!

Behold, your King is coming!

Zechariah 9:9

55

> Jesus answered and said to [Peter], "What I am doing, you do not understand now, but *you will know after this.*"
>
> JOHN 13:7

Just before Jesus washed the disciples' feet, the twelve were arguing over which of them was the greatest (Luke 22:17–30). Alas, that unnecessary debate goes on today because we have forgotten that Jesus alone is to have preeminence (Col. 1:18). Our Lord's actions that evening must have stunned these men, but he taught them a significant lesson that we all need to learn. *Unless we allow Jesus to minister to us, we are not prepared to minister for him to others.* Too many Christians trust their ministry success to their knowledge, education, training, and experience, or to their love for their people, and certainly these things are essential—but there are also other matters to consider if we are to serve Jesus effectively.

We don't know everything. "For we know in part" (1 Cor. 13:9), and if we are missing parts, we cannot complete the puzzle or build the machine. The twelve disciples had much more to learn about Jesus and so do we, but we also need to learn more about ourselves. Peter was certain that he could die for Jesus, but he soon discovered he was too weak even to admit he was one of Jesus's disciples (John 13:36–38). He tried to keep Jesus from going to the cross (Matt. 16:21–23) and recklessly used his sword to "protect" him. He even commanded Jesus not to wash his feet. If our ministry is based only on our limited knowledge and experience, we are unprepared to serve. We need to allow Jesus to show us what to do and how to do it.

What we do know, we must obey. The first disciples whose feet Jesus washed permitted him to do so and said nothing, but Peter protested (John 13:5–9). Washing people's feet was a menial task for the lowest servants, and Jesus was their Lord and the Son of God. When he told Peter he was going to wash his feet, Peter should have said, "Your will be done, Master." Instead, he refused to cooperate, first by pulling back his feet and then by asking for a complete bath—from one extreme to another, and both of them wrong. Jesus had taught them that obedience leads to more knowledge (7:17), so it's no surprise that Peter was so wrong.

We must follow our Lord's example and obey from a loving and humble heart. "Knowledge puffs up while love builds up" (1 Cor. 8:1 TNIV). When you read Peter's two epistles, you will find him writing frequently about love and knowledge. If our lives are to be constructive and glorify God, the Holy Spirit must guide us with spiritual knowledge and motivate us by the love of God in our hearts. Both of these blessings come from a faithful daily walk with the Lord. If we lack spiritual truth and love, we will be asking, "*How* can I get out of this?" instead of, "*What* can I get out of this for God's glory?" With each act of love and obedience, our love and knowledge will grow and the Spirit will build us up. Immature love is protective ("Lord, are *you* going to wash *my* feet?") and can take us out of God's will, while maturing love is obedient and says, "Your will be done, your name be glorified."

Jesus demonstrated the correct spiritual posture we must maintain: the bent knees of humility, the busy hands of service, the surrendered will of obedience, and the renewed mind of spiritual knowledge. The result will be the happy heart of the balanced believer. "If you know these things, blessed are you if you do them" (John 13:17). If we want to be great in the eyes of God, we must be the least in the eyes of men (Luke 22:24–27).

> For who is greater, he who sits at the table, or he who serves? Is it not he who sits at the table? Yet I am among you as the One who serves.
>
> Luke 22:27

56

[The Father will give you] the Spirit of truth, whom the world cannot receive, because it neither sees Him nor knows Him; but you know Him, for He dwells with you *and will be in you.*

JOHN 14:17

The believer's union with Christ through the Holy Spirit is a foundational truth that must be emphasized. Phrases such as "in Christ" and "in him" are used 164 times in the New Testament. Unless we abide in Christ, who dwells in us by his Spirit, we can do nothing (John 15:5). It's good to have training, education, giftedness, and zeal, but they accomplish nothing if we are trusting them instead of yielding to the Spirit. The Holy Spirit had been *with* the disciples in their Master, but the Spirit would fill each of them personally on the Day of Pentecost and baptize them into the body of Christ (Acts 1:5; 2:4; 1 Cor. 12:13).

Consider first *the Spirit and Jesus Christ.* He was conceived by the Spirit in Mary's virgin womb (Luke 1:35) and grew up under the Spirit's care (2:52). When he began his ministry at the age of thirty, the Holy Spirit empowered him for his daily life and ministry (Matt. 3:16–17; John 3:34). Daily he communed with the Father, meditated on the Word of God, spent time in prayer, and followed the Spirit's leading in what he did and said. He did not use his divine powers for himself but for the benefit of others. The Holy Spirit helped him when he was arrested, beaten, and crucified (Heb. 9:14), and the Spirit participated in his resurrection (Rom. 1:4; 1 Pet. 3:18). If our Lord in all his perfection needed the ministry of the Spirit to accomplish the Father's will, how much more do we disciples need him!

Now consider *the Spirit and the believer.* The identifying mark of a true believer is the presence of the Holy Spirit, who ministers to the believer just as Jesus did to the disciples. "Now if anyone does not have the Spirit of Christ, he is not His" (Rom. 8:9). If we have the Spirit, we will read the Scriptures with understanding and have a desire to obey them. We rejoice at the privilege of worshiping the Lord and fellowshiping with the saints. We feel "at home" in a Bible study or a prayer meeting, and we want to share Christ with others. Jesus taught his followers and the Spirit teaches us (John 16:12–15). Jesus prayed for them (and intercedes for us today) and the Spirit also intercedes for us (Rom. 8:26–27). Jesus gave power and authority to his disciples (Luke 9:1) and the Spirit enables believers today to serve the Lord (Acts 1:8). The Spirit has made each believer's body a temple of the Holy Spirit (1 Cor. 6:19–20) and the members of the body tools with which to serve the Lord (Rom. 6:12–13). The Spirit longs to make us more and more like Jesus (2 Cor. 3:18).

Finally, consider *the Spirit and the believer in the world*. The world cannot grasp who the Spirit is and what he does, because the mind of the unsaved person is blind to spiritual truth (1 Cor. 2:14–16) and understands only what can be seen, weighed, and handled. At Pentecost, the Spirit both filled the believers and baptized them into the body of Christ (Acts 1:5; 2:4; 1 Cor. 12:13). It is through the ministry and witness of God's people that the Spirit brings conviction to the lost and leads them to Christ. We must demonstrate God's love and share God's truth, and be salt and light in the world. Only the Spirit of truth can overcome the spirit of this world (1 Cor. 2:12) and bring sinners to the Savior, and the Spirit must use us to be witnesses.

We must stay on good terms with the Holy Spirit and not grieve him (Eph. 4:30), lie to him (Acts 5:3), resist him (7:51), or quench him (1 Thess. 5:19). If our goal in life is to glorify Jesus Christ, the Holy Spirit will help us, for that is his ministry (John 16:14).

He who is in you is greater than he who is in the world.

1 John 4:4

57

These things I have spoken to you, that My joy
may remain in you, and that *your joy may be full*.

JOHN 15:11

The disciples were in deep sorrow, but Jesus spoke to them about joy! He even called it "My joy." Knowing what was about to happen, how could he have joy? But that's the remarkable thing about the Christian life: the things that bring pain and sorrow can at the same time bring the joy of the Lord. Don't try to explain it, but do, by the Spirit, seek to experience it. Jesus compared his joy to a woman giving birth: the same baby that causes pain also brings the joy (John 16:21–22). Sometimes God removes pain, but often he transforms pain into the "birth" of joyful blessing. We are "more than conquerors through Him who loved us" (Rom. 8:37).

Fullness of joy should come from our worship of the Lord. "Rejoice in the Lord always. Again I will say, rejoice" (Phil. 4:4). Certainly we can rejoice in the person of the Lord, for each of his divine attributes means blessing and help for us. Simply meditating on the character of God, his works, his promises, the bright future he is preparing for us, and the opportunity of knowing and serving him, ought to fill us with joy. Prayer itself is a source of great joy (John 16:24), even if the Lord doesn't always answer as we had hoped.

But being worshipers is not enough. If we want fullness of joy, we must also be workers. "Do not sorrow, for the joy of the LORD is your strength" (Neh. 8:10). Circumstances in Nehemiah's day were dangerous and difficult, but the work was completed. Jesus saw the will of God as nourishment, not punishment (John 4:34). He endured the awful sufferings of Calvary "for the joy that was set before Him" (Heb. 12:2). Like him, we can "rejoice in hope of the glory of God" and see tribulations turned into triumphs (Rom. 5:1–5). "Those who sow in tears shall reap in joy. He who continually goes forth weeping, bearing seed for sowing, shall doubtless come again with rejoicing, bringing his sheaves with him" (Ps. 126:5–6; *see* Gal. 6:9).

Every Christian is a warrior. We have enemies to fight and battles to win, and the Lord is able to turn battles into blessings. "The LORD is my strength and my shield; my heart trusted in Him, and I am helped; therefore my heart greatly rejoices, and with my song I will praise Him" (Ps. 28:7). We have joy because of victory, but we cannot have victories without battles. Jesus has already overcome our three enemies—the world (John 16:33), the devil (Col. 2:13–15), and the flesh (Rom. 6:1–4)—so we fight *from his victories*. No matter what the enemy may be, it is faith in the Lord that gives us the victory (1 John 5:4).

Another source of joy is our hope in the Lord. The future is our friend when Jesus is our Lord, and we should be "rejoicing in hope, patient in tribulation" (Rom. 12:12). Joy is not an emotion that we manufacture; it is a living fruit that the Spirit produces in response to our faith. Until our Lord returns, we must walk by faith, trusting his promises in spite of the circumstances around us, the feelings within us, and the consequences before us.

Happiness depends on happenings, but joy depends on the power, promises, and providence of God. "But the fruit of the Spirit is love, joy, [and] peace" (Gal. 5:22). We can walk into each new day singing, "This is the day the LORD has made; we will rejoice and be glad in it" (Ps. 118:24). Jesus sang those words before he went out to Gethsemane (Matt. 26:30). Have we learned to sing them?

> Now may the God of hope fill you with all joy and peace in believing, that you may abound in hope by the power of the Holy Spirit.
>
> Romans 15:13

58

When He has come, *He will convict the world* of sin, and of righteousness, and of judgment.

JOHN 16:8

I f, in the upper room, you had measured the apostles by the world's standards, you would have concluded that they were unprepared to carry on the work of Christ. But in his high priestly prayer, Jesus told the Father they *were* prepared! "I have finished the work which You have given Me to do" (John 17:4), he said, and that work included teaching and training the apostles for their life ministries. Jesus had not only taught them God's Word, but he had also taught them how to pray, and he had been their example as a compassionate servant. Only one element was missing: the Holy Spirit, who alone could empower them to know and do God's will. The Holy Spirit was to be to the apostles what Jesus had been to them, and the Spirit would always be in them to enable them to live and labor for God's glory. Of itself, the church cannot save sinners or change the world, but the Holy Spirit can as he works in and through the church. Through our gracious words, our godly lives, and our good works, we can be the witnesses, and the Spirit will use our witness to bring conviction to the hearts of the lost concerning sin, righteousness, and judgment (16:8–11).

The world's greatest sin is *unbelief*: sinners have not trusted Jesus Christ, and this is why they are lost. Conscience may convict a person of sins, but only the Spirit can convict them of the greatest sin—rejecting Jesus Christ. A person may abandon both the sins of the flesh and of the spirit (2 Cor. 7:1) and still be lost, for it is only faith in Christ that gives new birth into the family of God. Peter preached Christ to the religious Jews at the feast of Pentecost and they were "cut to the heart" and cried out for help (Acts 2:37). The Spirit used the Word of God

120

to convict them. God's people are witnesses, not prosecuting attorneys, so let's leave the convicting to the Holy Spirit.

The lost world's greatest need is *the righteousness of Jesus Christ*. Whether they knew it or not, the people who watched Jesus serve on earth were beholding righteousness in action. Lost sinners cannot be saved by the righteousness of the law of Moses (Gal. 2:16–21), nor can their own self-righteousness save them (Isa. 64:6). Jesus knew no sin and did no sin (1 Pet. 2:22) because in him there was no sin (1 John 3:5). Jesus was willing to become sin for us (2 Cor. 5:21) that we might be clothed in his righteousness and "accepted in the Beloved" (Eph. 1:6). But Jesus has returned to heaven, so how can lost people see his righteousness and discover what they are missing? By seeing Jesus in the lives of his people (Matt. 5:13–16) and hearing Christ declared from the Word.

The lost world is under bondage to the devil, the prince of this world (Eph. 2:1–3), and its greatest need is *freedom from sin, death, and judgment*. Yet sinners rejoice in what they think is freedom. In his death and resurrection, Jesus won the greatest victory in history, defeating sin, death, and the devil. Jesus said, "Now is the judgment of this world; now the ruler of this world will be cast out" (John 12:31). To the unbelieving world, the cross looks like shameful defeat; but in reality, the cross is a glorious triumph (Col. 2:15). When Jesus died, he did not whisper, "I am finished!" He shouted, "It is finished!" The work of redemption had been completed!

If the Holy Spirit is to bring conviction to the hearts of lost people, God's people must be available to him, manifesting the fruit of the Spirit in their lives (Gal. 5:22–23) and sharing the good news. Let's be faithful witnesses, telling "the truth, the whole truth, and nothing but the truth," and trusting the Holy Spirit to do the rest. He is willing. Are we?

For we cannot but speak the things which we have seen and heard.

Acts 4:20

59

> These things I have spoken to you, that in Me you may have peace. In the world you will have tribulation; but be of good cheer, *I have overcome the world*.

JOHN 16:33

"These things" refer to the truths Jesus had just taught the disciples in the upper room, truths that we must lay hold of today. He climaxed the discourse with this word of encouragement that must have strengthened the disciples many times as they served and suffered in the years that followed. He reveals three important truths that we must grasp.

The opposition that will be against us. The word *world* has three meanings in Scripture: the created world (Acts 17:24), the world of people (John 3:16), and the whole system of society that is apart from God and at enmity with God (16:33). Satan is the prince of this world system (12:31) and uses it to entice and enslave people so that they will live for the temporary and not for the eternal. First John 2:15–17 informs us that anything that decreases our love for the Father or our desire to do his will is from the world and must be avoided, no matter how good it may seem to us or to others. We must not be shocked when we are attacked by the world, because Christians don't belong to this world (John 17:14–15; 1 Pet. 4:12–19). If our Christian life is what it ought to be, the world will treat us as it treated Jesus. If we are friends of the world, we cannot be the friends of God (James 4:4).

The peace and joy that should be within us. If we have war on the outside, it's essential to have peace on the inside, otherwise we will be overcome and not overcomers. "Be anxious for nothing, but in everything by prayer and supplication, with thanksgiving, let your requests be made known to God; and the peace of God, which surpasses all understanding, will guard your hearts and minds through Christ Jesus" (Phil. 4:6–7). Tribulation is as important to the Christian life as the sun is to plant life, for it develops character and helps to make us more like Christ as we share "the fellowship of His sufferings" (3:10). The potter not only molds the vessel but he also puts it into the furnace to make it useable. When Jesus says "be of good cheer," it isn't just a passing phrase like "have a good day." It's a gift of joy we can experience now. "Son, be of good cheer; your sins are forgiven you" (Matt. 9:2). "Be of good cheer! It is I; do not be afraid" (14:27). Why shouldn't we have peace and joy? Jesus is with us, we are forgiven, and he has already overcome the enemy.

The victory that is already before us. During his earthly ministry, Jesus defeated Satan time and time again, and in his crucifixion, resurrection, and ascension, he conquered the enemy once and for all (Col. 2:15; Eph. 1:19–23). The Lamb has overcome the serpent (Gen. 3:15; Rev. 5:5; 12:11) and by faith, we share in his victory. Jesus is the strong man who overcame the devil and stripped him of his armor (Luke 11:22). The Father wants us to be like those young men John wrote to who had "overcome the wicked one" (1 John 2:13; *see* Rev. 12:11). When Joshua led the Jewish army from victory to victory, conquering the Promised Land, they simply obeyed God's will, trusted God's promise, and overcame the enemy. "Do not fear or be dismayed," God said to his people, "for the LORD is with you" (2 Chron. 20:17). This does not mean we are spectators and not combatants, for we must put on the armor, take the sword and shield (Eph. 6:10–20), and resist the devil, trusting Jesus because of the victory he has already won.

Are we overcomers or overcome?

Be strong in the Lord and in the power of His might.

Ephesians 6:10

60

I have glorified You on the earth. *I have finished the work* which You have given Me to do.

JOHN 17:4

From the day of his baptism to the day of his burial, Jesus lived in the same manner you and I must live today: trusting the Father, feeding on the Scriptures, praying, and depending on the Holy Spirit. He lived by faith. Satan tempted him to use his powers for his own comfort, but Jesus refused. He had laid aside the independent use of his divine attributes (Phil. 2:5–11). He patiently bore with the limitations of a human body and the frustrations of a human society, including the hypocrisy and unbelief of the religious leaders, the trials and tears of the common people, and their sicknesses and sins. He was moved with compassion for these sheep who had no shepherd. But there were also happy times, when parents brought their children to him for his blessing and when he was invited to a neighborhood wedding with his mother and his disciples. He brought light to the blind, love to the rejected, and life to the dead. He did the Father's work and glorified the Father.

What was this work? For one thing, he *revealed the Father* (John 14:7–11). To see Jesus was to see the Father. Many of the people saw God only as a King who made rules and punished offenders. Jesus showed them a Father who loved them, provided for them, and heard their prayers and answered them. Jesus hugged the children and touched the lepers. Is God like that? Yes!

His work also involved *fulfilling Old Testament prophecies.* The Old Testament was systematically read in the synagogues and the temple, and the rabbis taught the people that the Messiah was coming. But when he came, they did not accept him. "You search the Scriptures," Jesus told the crowd, "for in them you think you have eternal life; and these are they which testify of Me" (5:39). What a joy it is to meet Jesus in the pages of the Old Testament! When he healed the sick and injured and raised the dead, he was fulfilling the Old Testament prophecies. You often find in the four Gospels the phrase "that the Scripture might be fulfilled."

Another ministry of Jesus was *setting an example for us to follow*. Making Jesus our example does not save us, but it should announce to others that we belong to Jesus and want to live as he lived (1 Pet. 2:21–25). How did he treat his enemies? How did he relate to the outcasts, to the Roman soldiers and officials, and to the people who crucified him? How should we relate to civil government? Jesus is the example to follow.

Of course, the major reason he came was *to be the sacrifice for our sins*. "And as Moses lifted up the serpent in the wilderness, even so must the Son of Man be lifted up, that whoever believes in Him should not perish but have eternal life" (John 3:14–15). The Jewish people had the law of Moses, the temple, the priesthood, and the sacrifices, each of which pointed to Jesus Christ but did not provide salvation. The law made nothing perfect (Heb. 7:19) and neither did the priesthood (v. 11), nor the sacrifices (9:9; 10:1), *but Jesus does* (13:20–21). We are "complete in Him" (Col. 2:10). By one offering he has perfected us forever (Heb. 10:14).

He trained his disciples to take his place (John 17:6–19). When the Spirit endued them with power at Pentecost (Acts 1:8), they were ready to bear witness of Jesus. We need to train new believers in the Bible and in how to live for Jesus and serve him. All of us need to be praying daily, "Father, help me to glorify you and to finish the work you have given me to do. Help me to end well."

That the name of our Lord Jesus Christ may be glorified in you, and you in Him.

2 Thessalonians 1:12

61

> Now I am no longer in this world, but these are in the world, and I come to You. Holy Father, keep through Your name those whom You have given Me, *that they may be one* as We are.
>
> JOHN 17:11

Six times in this wonderful prayer, our Lord used the word *one* as he prayed for the unity of the church (John 17:11, 21, 22, 23). Jesus is not asking for a gigantic man-made organization that promotes uniformity but a spiritual oneness like that of the Godhead, a oneness he called "one in Us" (v. 21; *see* v. 23). Not only does this unity enrich the church and enable it to minister, but it is also a witness to the lost world of the reality of the Savior and of the Father's love. Divided churches and disputing Christians are not very good witnesses to the love of God and the glory of the Son. Consider the "ties that bind" God's people together.

We have God's life, eternal life. The world is dead in sin and falling apart (Eph. 2:1), but believers are alive in Christ, sharing the very life of God. Whether vegetable, animal, or human, the bodies of things that are alive stay together, but when they die, plants wither and crumble and the corpses of animals and people decay and turn to dust. Death divides but life unites. Even though we who are in the family of God share the life of God, there is still diversity in God's family just as there is diversity in the members of the human body or a human family. If you and I belong to the family of God, we have the same Father and share the same spiritual life, and we ought to be able to live together and work together to the glory of God.

We share God's love. Jesus asked the Father "that the love with which You loved Me may be in them, and I in them" (John 17:26). The Father loves each of his children just as he loves his own Son! No love is greater. How many times do parents say to their children, "Can't you love one another?" Uniformity comes from pressure on the outside—the command of a general, the order of a boss—but unity comes from love on the inside, God's love implanted by the Holy Spirit. Have you read 1 Corinthians 13 lately? I hear this "love chapter" read at wedding ceremonies, but it was written to be read *and obeyed* at church business meetings.

We share God's glory. No matter what our physique, our clothing, or our appearance, every child of God already has God's glory within (John 17:22). As we grow in godliness, the glory gets greater (2 Cor. 3:18) and God is glorified more and more. Christians can love other believers because Christ lives in them, and we can love the lost because Christ died for them. One day in heaven we shall behold Christ's glory (John 17:24). Since all of God's children will be together in heaven, can't we learn to live and work together today? What a witness that is to a lost world!

We share God's truth (vv. 8, 14, 17). If we love God's Word, receive it into our hearts, and obey it, we will be peacemakers and not troublemakers. According to John's second epistle, we are expected to know the truth (2 John 1), have the truth abiding in us (v. 2), love in truth (v. 3), and walk in the truth (v. 4). Pride divides, but the Word of God humbles us and encourages unity. Lies open the door to Satan, but the truth keeps him at bay.

We share God's commission. Two phrases define our task: "that the world may believe" (John 17:21) and "that the world may know" (v. 23). A united church is an army of evangelists reaping the harvest together. The people in a divided church use the sickles on each other and lose the harvest. Shall we help answer our Lord's prayer "that they may be one"?

> For as the body is one and has many members, but all the members of that one body, being many, are one body, so also is Christ. For by one Spirit we were all baptized into one body.
>
> 1 Corinthians 12:12–13

62

Sanctify them by Your truth. Your word is truth.

JOHN 17:17

In the Christian vocabulary, "to sanctify" means "to set apart for God's exclusive service." Jesus has set himself apart to serve us as intercessor and high priest (John 17:19), and we should set ourselves apart to serve him. "And do not be conformed to this world, but be transformed by the renewing of your mind, that you may prove what is that good and acceptable and perfect will of God" (Rom. 12:2). That transformation takes place in our inner person as the Spirit of God uses the Word of God to make us more like Jesus (2 Cor. 3:18). In the Greek text, the word *world* is used eighteen times in John 17, and it means the "world system" or "society without God," all that pressures us to be like sinners and not like Christ. Three fundamental facts stand out.

God's people do not belong to the world. We are *in* the world but not *of* the world. Anything that causes us to stop enjoying the Father's love or doing the Father's will is of the world and is wrong for us (1 John 2:15–17). But neither is separation from the world isolation from the world, for we are here to witness and to serve. Jesus was the friend of publicans and sinners and yet was "holy, harmless, undefiled, separate from sinners" (Heb. 7:26). Separation is not insulation, having no compassion for the lost and keeping them at arm's length. When we start imitating the world and seeking to please the world, then we are in trouble. "Demas has forsaken me, having loved this present world," wrote Paul (2 Tim. 4:10).

God's people are different from the world. Our citizenship is in heaven (Phil. 3:20) and we seek to please our Father in heaven (Matt. 6:9). Practical godliness sets us apart from the rest of the world and what it has to offer. Note that I said *different*, not *odd* or *weird*. When we are different we attract people, but when we are odd we repel them; our calling is to attract people to Jesus. We follow his example of love and service and seek to do good to others. "Let your light so shine before men, that they may see your good works and glorify your Father in heaven" (Matt. 5:16). The world thrives on lies, but believers are sanctified by the truth—not just truth but *the* truth, the very essence of what is true. Jesus is the truth (John 14:6), the Spirit is the truth (1 John 5:6), the Word of God is the truth (John 17:17), and the church is "the pillar and ground of the truth" (1 Tim. 3:15). It is God's truth that makes us different from the world and is one reason why the world hates us (John 17:14).

God's people are in the world to win the lost to Jesus Christ. Jesus prayed, "As you sent me into the world, I also have sent them into the world" (v. 18). If Christians would just remember that they are representing Jesus Christ before a watching world, it would help them do what is right. We are salt (Matt. 5:13), and salt makes people thirsty.

God will one day take us out of this world! Jesus wants his church to be in heaven with him forever (John 17:24), and he has promised, "I will come again" (14:1–3). Meanwhile, he is our great high priest in heaven, interceding for us, hearing our prayers, and providing all we need as we seek to serve him. The world is our enemy (James 4:4), but in his death, burial, resurrection, ascension, and enthronement, Jesus has overcome the world (John 16:33) and we are "more than conquerors through Him who loved us" (Rom. 8:37).

And this is the victory that has overcome the world—our faith.

1 John 5:4

63

Jesus answered, "I have told you that I am He. Therefore, if you seek Me, *let these go their way*."

JOHN 18:8

Sometimes a crisis makes a person, but always a crisis shows what a person is made of. As he prayed to his Father, Jesus transformed the garden of Gethsemane into a holy of holies, but Judas and the official detachment tried to turn it into a battleground. (And Peter helped!) However, there is no question that Jesus was in charge. Why? Because he had been on his face in the garden, praying to the Father and surrendering to his will. The intruders had weapons in their hands, but Jesus had the cup from the Father in his hand and had prayed, "Your will be done." Because he had accepted the cup, Jesus was able to handle the people and the circumstances in the garden that critical night.

Jesus was able to approach the detachment with courage. Jesus knew what was going to happen (John 18:4) and went forward to meet the men. Before they could say anything, he asked, "Whom are you seeking?" "Jesus of Nazareth," they replied, and he calmly said, "I am He" (v. 5). Our Lord's words and fearless demeanor stunned the detachment and "they drew back and fell to the ground" (v. 6). He asked a second time and got the same answer. It's obvious that Jesus was in control of the meeting. He surrendered himself to them and asked that they let the men with him go their own way. Our Lord willingly surrendered himself so that his disciples could go free. The Holy Spirit gave the disciples this same courageous confidence as they ministered in the early days of the church, and it amazed their persecutors (Acts 4:13–41).

Jesus was able to confront Judas. Our Lord was not surprised that Judas had betrayed him, for he had known all along that the treasurer of the group was a counterfeit (John 6:67–71). It's a difficult thing to confront a devil, a dishonest thief and liar, without wanting to retaliate, but Jesus only quietly rebuked Judas for the counterfeit kiss. Peter would have killed Judas, but Jesus knew that Judas's sins would find him out.

Jesus was able to reprove Peter. Jesus shows the courage and love that come from submission, and Peter shows the folly that comes from sinful anger. In the garden he denied Jesus with his sword, and a few hours later he denied Jesus with words. Yet he had boasted that he would lay down his life for the Master! Once again, Peter tried to keep Jesus from obeying the Father's will and going to the cross. Peter needed to learn that Christians use spiritual weapons for fighting the devil and his servants (2 Cor. 10:4).

Jesus was able to protect the disciples. This is the key idea behind these events, that the detachment of soldiers and officials allowed the disciples to go free. Jesus had warned the men that, boasting or no boasting, they would forsake him, and he based it on Zechariah 13:7, "Strike the Shepherd, and the sheep will be scattered" (*see* Matt. 26:31). Not until the Holy Spirit empowered them would the disciples be prepared for persecution. Disobeying orders, Peter followed the Lord and got into deep trouble. Jesus not only keeps us *saved* (John 10:28), but he also keeps us *safe* if we are in his will (17:12).

The name *Gethsemane* means "oil press," and Jesus was about to go through indescribable suffering as he was tried, beaten, and crucified. But he came through triumphantly, as he said he would, and he is able to lead us to victory in our difficult circumstances *if we have accepted the cup and submitted to God's will*. Let him have his way and pray, "Not my will, but your will be done." If we take the cup, we need not fear what the sword can do.

Are you able to drink the cup that I am about to drink?

Matthew 20:22

64

> Pilate therefore said to Him, "*Are You a king then?*" Jesus answered, "You say rightly that I am a king."

JOHN 18:37

Paul tells us that Jesus "witnessed the good confession before Pontius Pilate" (1 Tim. 6:13), a confession of kingship that is found in all four Gospels. Jesus did not say, "I will be a king," but, "I am a king."

Jesus was born a king. "Where is He who has been born King of the Jews?" asked the magi (Matt. 2:2), and they were led to Jesus in Bethlehem. Pilate must have been perplexed when Jesus said he was "born" (his humanity) and also that he "came into this world" (his deity). Every other baby is "in the world" from conception, but Jesus had to "come into the world" to be conceived in Mary's womb. He is the King of glory (Ps. 24:7–10), King of Israel (John 1:49), King of kings (1 Tim. 6:15; Rev. 17:14), and King of the saints (Rev. 15:3).

Jesus served as king. Though he had left his throne and become a servant, Jesus was still king and used his authority to serve others. He commanded animals, fish, birds, rain, wind, and waves; he conquered the devil, demons, diseases, disabilities, and death itself. Most important, his kingdom is a kingdom of truth and he is able to overcome Satan's kingdom of lies and set people free. The world has rejected him and his kingdom of truth, but you and I are his servants, and wherever we are, the kingdom of God has arrived.

Jesus died as king. "JESUS OF NAZARETH, KING OF THE JEWS," read the placard nailed to the cross over his head (John 19:19). His robe was taken from him by gambling soldiers and his crown was a crown of thorns. Instead of shouting "God save the king," the people ridiculed him. Yet Jesus reigned from the cross! He prayed for the Jewish leaders and the Roman soldiers. He brought a repentant criminal into his kingdom. He commanded John to care for Mary, his mother. He defeated Satan and the hosts of hell, brought darkness for three hours as he atoned for the sins of the world, caused an earthquake, opened graves and raised the dead, and finished the work he had come to do. No wonder Christians everywhere glory in the cross (Gal. 6:14).

Jesus reigns today! Since his ascension to heaven, Jesus is enthroned as our Priest-King "according to the order of Melchizedek" (Heb. 6:20; *see* Gen. 14:18–24). The name *Melchizedek* means "king of righteousness." Nowhere in Scripture do we find the offices of king and priest united except in Jesus. He reigns from a throne of grace to which we have access (Heb. 4:14–16) and he has all authority in heaven and on earth (Matt. 28:18). As our High Priest, he feels our pains and knows our needs, and as our King, he is able to give to us and do for us all that is best.

Jesus will return and reign on earth. On that day, every knee shall bow and every tongue confess that Jesus Christ is Lord (Phil. 2:9–11). The whole world will acknowledge that he is King of kings and Lord of lords (Rev. 19:16). Those who have trusted him will reign with him and serve him forever and ever (22:5). The assignments he gives us will depend on how we have served him in our lives today. Have we been faithful and obedient? Have we sought to glorify him? Those who have rejected him will be cast into outer darkness to suffer forever.

Is Jesus the King in your life and mine? Does he govern us by his truth? Are we serving him and seeking to win others? May the Lord help us to be ready when Jesus returns!

> Just and true are Your ways,
> O King of the saints!
>
> Revelation 15:3

65

From then on Pilate sought to release Him, but the
Jews cried out saying "If you let this Man go, *you
are not Caesar's friend*. Whoever makes himself
a king speaks against Caesar."

JOHN 19:12

Pontius Pilate, the Roman governor of Judea, is mentioned fifty-five times in the New Testament. His name
is also spoken by millions of Christians around the
world when they express their faith by saying the Apostles'
Creed: "he suffered under Pontius Pilate." The Romans were
known for excellence in warfare, organization, and adminis-
tration, and their administrators knew how to play the game of
politics. Someone has said that a statesman is concerned about
the next generation, while a politician is concerned about the
next election. Pilate was concerned about *Pilate*, which
meant getting along with the Jewish people and staying in
office.

Encouraged by the Jewish religious leaders, *the crowd
shouted some false accusations against Jesus*. They told Pilate
Jesus was an evildoer who stirred up the people (John 18:30;
Luke 23:1–5). But Jesus never meddled in politics, and when
his enemies tried to trap him with trick questions about paying taxes to Caesar, his reply shut their mouths. They told
Pilate that Jesus said he was the Son of God, an accusation
that shook the governor but generated no action. Religion
was not Pilate's forte. Finally the religious leaders pushed the
right button: "He claims to be a king! We have no king but
Caesar!" Politics was something Pilate did understand, and
angry mobs challenging his leadership were something that
he feared. "If you let Jesus of Nazareth go free, you are not
Caesar's friend!" they told him.

The governor made some bad decisions. Pilate knew that the Jewish religious leaders were envious of Jesus's popularity, amazing powers, and ability to teach wisdom (Matt. 27:18). The governor sought for legal ways to set Jesus free, but to no avail. When Pilate learned that Jesus was from Galilee, he sent him to King Herod, but Herod only sent him back to Pilate. Herod was a shrewd politician in his own right. However, you cannot let other people make decisions about Jesus that you must make for yourself. Only you can answer life's most important question: "What then shall I do with Jesus who is called Christ?" (v. 22). Pilate was a double-minded man and therefore unstable in all his ways (James 4:8). He wanted to please the Jews while at the same time not arousing the anger and disapproval of the emperor. Double-minded people are also double-tongued (1 Tim. 3:8), and they falter from one wrong decision to another (1 Kings 18:21). They also have double vision and lack that singlehearted obedience that puts Jesus first in everything (Col. 1:18). Believers are friends of Jesus Christ (John 15:13–15), and pleasing him governs everything.

Jesus made a good confession. Paul wrote that "Christ Jesus . . . witnessed the good confession before Pontius Pilate" (1 Tim. 6:13). Paul was encouraging Timothy to be a courageous Christian, unafraid of what the lost world says or does. The leaders of Israel disowned their own Messiah and delivered him up to be crucified (Acts 3:13; 4:27), but Jesus used his suffering as an opportunity to bear witness to the truth. Peter commands believers to follow our Lord's example (1 Pet. 4:12–19). If Jesus is our friend, we will stand up for him no matter what the crowd may shout. Pilate wanted both Tiberius Caesar and the Jewish crowd to be his friends, and that decision cost him everything. The King of kings is our friend!

You are My friends if you do whatever I command you.

John 15:14

66

So when Jesus had received the sour wine, *He said, "It is finished!"* And bowing His head, He gave up His spirit.

JOHN 19:30

What is finished? The work of atonement! "It is finished" is one Greek word, ten letters long, and the perfect tense may be translated, "it has been finished, it stands finished today, and it always will be finished." The costly work of atonement was accomplished by Jesus in six painful hours on the cross and we dare add nothing to it. Jesus paid it all; he did not make a down payment and expect us to keep up installments. Before he was arrested, Jesus said to his Father, "I have glorified You on the earth. I have finished the work which You have given Me to do" (John 17:4). Every believer should want to be able to say that to the Father on arriving in heaven. I have learned so much from the way Jesus did the Father's work here on earth.

To begin with, *each believer has an appointed work to do*. "For we are His workmanship, created in Christ Jesus for good works, which God prepared beforehand that we should walk in them" (Eph. 2:10). Not only did God prepare the works for us, but he also prepared us to be able to do them. Our abilities, interests, experiences, spiritual gifts, and growing knowledge of God and the Bible are blended to equip us to become workers who need not be ashamed (2 Tim. 2:15). God has different ways of preparing his workers and often bypasses the training that our educators think is essential. If we are willing to obey, God will show us what he wants us to do (John 7:17).

The Lord not only chooses and equips us, but he *also has a plan for our lives*. The next time you read John's Gospel, note how often "the hour" is mentioned. Jesus spent his first thirty years on earth in Nazareth. At the right time, he was baptized by John the Baptist, tempted in the wilderness by Satan, and began his public ministry. He called four fishermen to become disciples and later added others to be trained to work with him. Early each morning, Jesus went to a solitary place to pray and receive his "orders of the day" from the Father (Isa. 50:4–7). When it comes to doing God's will on schedule, we must not be like horses that rush ahead or mules that lag behind (Ps. 32:8–9). Can we honestly say to the Father, "My times are in Your hand" (31:15)? How can we claim Romans 8:28 if we are not in the Father's will?

Most important, *we are here to serve, not to be served.* The twelve apostles often debated among themselves which of them was the greatest, and Jesus had to remind them that they were chosen to serve others, just as he served others (Matt. 18:1–6). The night Jesus was betrayed, the disciples came to the Passover feast arguing about greatness (Luke 22:24–30), and Jesus solved their problem by washing their feet! In the world, success is measured by how many people work for you, but in the kingdom, the test is "For how many do you work?" Christian service involves pain and sacrifice, disappointments and difficulties, and must be motivated by love alone.

I have often pondered the ministry of the apostle Paul—the burdens he carried, the battles he had to wage, the misunderstandings he had to untangle, the people he had to encourage, and the many sacrifices he had to make—and I have asked myself, *Could I have done that? In my own strength?* I must answer an emphatic "No!" But I can also say with Paul, "I can do all things through Christ who strengthens me" (Phil. 4:13). We serve a wonderful Master who knows us better than we know ourselves, and he gives us only those assignments that he has prepared for us and that he has prepared us for. What a joyful privilege it is to serve him!

> [Know] that from the Lord you will receive the reward of the inheritance; for you serve the Lord Christ.
>
> Colossians 3:24

67

> Jesus said to her, "*Woman, why are you weeping? Whom are you seeking?*"

JOHN 20:15

When God created the first man and woman, he gave them tear ducts that would help maintain the health of their eyes. Then they disobeyed God and brought sin into the world. Adam and Eve must have wept when they were evicted from the garden and when Abel was murdered by Cain. Today, when we are in physical pain or deep sorrow, weeping can be part of the healing process. Mary Magdalene owed everything to Jesus (Luke 8:1–2) and was greatly disturbed when she came to the garden and found the tomb open and the body gone. Let's consider the transformation she experienced because she met the risen Christ.

She arrived in the garden as *a mourner* (John 20:11). Her weeping was not quiet but rather the loud sobbing Jewish people displayed in those days. Her imagination was working overtime because she had concluded that somebody had taken away the body of Jesus. Counselors tell us that most of the difficulties people imagine never actually occur, or if they do occur are never as cataclysmic as imagined. Jesus had told his followers that he would be raised from the dead on the third day, but for some reason the message never registered in their minds. But before we condemn Mary and her friends, let's confess that we have also been disturbed by imaginary problems because we have forgotten God's promises or not claimed them. We serve a risen Savior and have a "living hope through the resurrection of Jesus Christ from the dead" (1 Pet. 1:3). The Christian life is a feast, not a funeral (1 Cor. 5:8). Mary was so blinded by grief that she did not recognize angels in the tomb or Jesus outside the tomb.

When Jesus came to her, Mary became *a manager*. She had the situation under control. If the gardener would show her where the corpse lay, she would take it away (John 20:15). When we are emotionally disturbed and jumping to conclusions, how easy it is for us to know exactly what God ought to do and offer to help him! Faith is living without scheming, and our feeble plans only make matters worse and hinder God from showing his power and receiving glory. Whenever I get into that kind of attitude, the Lord reminds me of Psalm 46:10—"Be still, and know that I am God." The Hebrew word translated "be still" also means "relax, take your hands off." God does not need my advice; he is much wiser than I am. What a mess we can make of God's work and our ministries by meddling with his plans! When Jesus spoke Mary's name, she recognized him and fell at his feet in worship, something that could have happened earlier had she remembered the promises Jesus gave.

Now Mary was *a messenger*. "Go to my brethren," Jesus commanded her, and off she went to the place where the disciples were meeting (John 20:17–18). "Come and see" and "Go and tell" are the two Easter commands for God's people to obey (Matt. 28:6–7). Jesus is alive! He has all authority and has defeated every enemy. Mary wanted to hold his feet and keep him for herself, but he told her to get on her feet and run with the message. What a privilege to bear the good news of the resurrection to a world desperate for hope!

Don't weep over a living and triumphant Christ. Weep over a dead and defeated church that does not know "the power of His resurrection" (Phil. 3:10). Do our lives and churches convince people that Jesus is alive? Or do we have a name that we are alive, but we are dead (Rev. 3:1)?

> Therefore let us celebrate the feast . . . with the unleavened bread of sincerity and truth.
>
> 1 Corinthians 5:8 NASB

68

Peter, seeing [John], said to Jesus, "But *Lord, what
about this man?*"

When Peter disagreed with Jesus about his going
to the cross, Jesus said, "Get behind Me, Satan!"
(Matt. 16:21–23). When Peter drew his sword in
the garden and cut off a man's ear, Jesus commanded him to
stop fighting and then healed the man (John 18:10–11; Luke
22:51). When Peter denied the Lord the third time, Jesus
calmly looked at him (Luke 22:60–62), and Peter went out
and wept bitterly. When after Christ's resurrection, Peter went
back to fishing and caught nothing, in the morning Jesus
gave him a great catch of fish and even served him breakfast
(John 21:1–14). But that same morning, when Peter began to
meddle with the will of God for the life of his friend John,
Jesus rebuked him and told him to mind his own business.

Following Jesus by seeking his will and obeying it is the
major privilege and responsibility of every Christian. No matter how many gifts and talents we think we possess or how
much experience we think we have had in Christian service,
if we fail to seek God's will and do it from the heart (Eph.
6:6), we are wasting our lives and accomplishing nothing
for the kingdom of God. It's good to encourage others to
obey God's will, but if we are not obeying it ourselves, our
concern is only hypocritical camouflage. Peter and John had
often worked together, and perhaps Peter was wondering if
that partnership would continue. They had been together at
Christ's transfiguration and at the raising of Jairus's daughter
from the dead. They had set up the Passover feast for Jesus
and the twelve and had been in the garden with Jesus when
he prayed. On resurrection morning, they had run together

to the tomb and found it empty. But no matter how many remarkable experiences we may have as we serve the Lord together, we must never meddle with the will of God for somebody else's life.

As I look back over sixty-plus years of Christian service, I recall the well-meaning people who thought they knew God's will for my life—the schools I should attend, whom I should marry, where I should serve—and I'm grateful I did not try to please them. I appreciated the love of those who warned me when I was about to make mistakes, but I didn't appreciate the "omniscience" of people when I was making decisions.

God guides us when we are willing to obey him. "If anyone wants to do his will," said Jesus, "he shall know concerning the doctrine, whether it is from God" (John 7:17). The will of God is not one of many options, as if it were part of a "religious buffet." God's will is the command of the King and it must be obeyed. Once we know God's will we must obey it, and in obeying we will discover even more about our God and his will. The will of God is the expression of the love of God for us, and we must keep our eyes on Jesus (Heb. 12:1–2). Peter started to follow Jesus and then looked back and saw John, and asked about the Lord's will for his life. He had made a similar mistake when walking on the water (Matt. 14:28–31). We keep our eyes on Jesus when we meditate on the Word of God and pray (Acts 6:4), when we obey the Lord in what we already know, and when we thank the Lord for the new truths he shows us. We appreciate the counsel of Christian friends, but John 21:22–23 warns us that even they can misunderstand the will of God! Remember Paul, Barnabas, and Mark (Acts 15:36–42; Col. 4:10; 2 Tim. 4:11).

Peter learned his lesson. Years later, he wrote, "But let none of you suffer as . . . a busybody in other people's matters" (1 Pet. 4:15).

[Look] unto Jesus, the author and finisher of our faith.

Hebrews 12:2

69

> *But you shall receive power* when the Holy Spirit
> has come upon you; and you shall be witnesses to
> Me in Jerusalem, and in all Judea and Samaria,
> and to the end of the earth.
>
> ACTS 1:8

The early church owned no buildings, had no big budgets
(Acts 3:6), and was made up primarily of common
people who had no influential friends "at the top."
And yet, those early believers fulfilled Christ's commission
and successfully carried the gospel to their world. Believers
today have means of transportation and communication that
would astound Peter and Paul, yet we are falling behind.
In fact, church growth in the United States is mainly from
people transferring their membership from one church to
another and not because brand-new believers are looking
for church homes.

We are commanded to be witnesses through both the way
we live and the words we speak. Witnesses are people who
tell others what they know about Jesus and what he has done
for them (4:20). They lovingly share the good news of salvation. Actually, all believers *are* witnesses, either good ones
or bad ones. Unfortunately, some are more like prosecuting
attorneys or judges and do very little witnessing. The Greek
word for "witness" gives us the English word *martyr*, and
many of the Lord's faithful witnesses have sealed their witness with their blood.

We cannot witness effectively without divine power. Jesus
commanded his disciples to stay in Jerusalem until they were
empowered by the Spirit (Luke 24:46–49), for only then would
they be equipped to communicate the gospel. You would think
that the believers who met in the upper room (Acts 1:12–14)

had everything they needed to evangelize Jerusalem. After all, they had known Jesus personally. The apostles had lived with Jesus and been taught by him. They had seen his miracles and even done miracles themselves. But they were still not ready to witness until they had the power of the Spirit, for it is the Spirit's ministry to equip us for service. *Our assets are liabilities apart from the ministry of the Spirit.*

In his upper room discourse (John 13–16), Jesus taught the disciples about the ministry of the Holy Spirit. The Spirit would help them know and do God's will (14:15–17) and would teach them the Scriptures and help them recall what they had learned (14:25–26; 16:13–15). He would give them power to witness (15:2–27) and would bring conviction to those who heard (16:7–11). This would result in Jesus being glorified (v. 14). The book of Acts records all of these ministries of the Spirit as demonstrated in the life of the early church. Do we see them in the churches today?

Because we have trusted Jesus Christ and received salvation, we have the Holy Spirit dwelling within us (Rom. 8:9), *but does the Holy Spirit have us?* When evangelist D. L. Moody was ministering in Great Britain, a critical minister asked, "Does Mr. Moody have a monopoly on the Holy Spirit?" A friend replied, "No, but the Holy Spirit has a monopoly on D. L. Moody." To be filled with the Spirit means to be controlled by the Spirit and willingly used by him to honor the Lord. I once heard A. W. Tozer say, "If God were to take the Holy Spirit out of this world, most of what the churches are doing would go right on *and nobody would know the difference.*" Do we know the difference?

> When the Helper comes, whom I shall send to you from the Father, the Spirit of truth who proceeds from the Father, He will testify of Me. And you also will bear witness.
>
> John 15:26–27

70

For it is written in the Book of Psalms: "Let his dwelling place be desolate, and let no one live in it"; and, "*Let another take his office.*"

ACTS 1:20

There were 120 believers, men and women, meeting in an upper room in Jerusalem, waiting for the coming of the promised Holy Spirit (Luke 24:49; Acts 1:8). This included the apostles, Mary the mother of Jesus, and our Lord's half-brothers. It was a prayer meeting that became a business meeting for the choosing of a new apostle. Let's focus our attention on three men.

First, let's consider *Peter the leader*. In every list in Scripture of the names of the apostles, Peter's name is always first, for Jesus selected him to be "the first among equals." Peter's failings during his years of training might suggest that he was not capable of leadership, but he was now equipped for the task. Though the baptism and filling of the Spirit would not occur until Pentecost, the apostles did have the presence of the Holy Spirit within (John 20:19–23), and their hearts had been opened to understand the Scriptures (Luke 24:44–45). God had shown Peter from Psalms 69:25 and 109:8 that a new apostle must be chosen to replace Judas. On Pentecost, the apostles would be witnessing to the twelve tribes of Israel, and their number had to be complete. (Note that Psalm 69 is a Messianic psalm.) Peter stated the qualifications for the apostle: (1) he had to have been with Jesus from the time of John's baptism, and (2) he had to have seen the risen Christ so he could bear witness of the resurrection (Acts 1:22). Two men were named, the group prayed, and the lots were cast. God's choice was Matthias, which means "gift of Jehovah." If every local church would depend on prayer and the Word

144

of God (6:4) and respect the leadership God has provided, there would be fewer church problems.

Now let's consider *Judas the traitor*. His name means "praise" but his life brought no glory to God. He was treasurer of the disciple group and stole money from the treasury (John 12:6). John 6:67–71 makes it clear that Judas was never born again but was a servant of the devil (13:21–30). However, the other eleven disciples did not know Judas was a counterfeit, and Jesus took pains not to expose him. From the parable of the tares (Matt. 13:24–30, 36–43) we learn that wherever God plants true children of God, the devil comes and plants counterfeits. Judas was the counterfeit in the disciple band. I think it was Charles Spurgeon who said, "If you want to make a devil, you must start with an angel; if you want to make a Judas, you must start with an apostle." Sad to say, there are counterfeits in every profession, but it is in the church that they do the most damage.

Finally, consider *Matthias the new apostle*. The fact that Matthias is never again mentioned in the Acts or the epistles says nothing about him or his ministry, for most of the original disciples are not mentioned outside the Gospels. God chose Matthias and therefore equipped him to do the work assigned to him. Not every Christian worker is famous, yet God's people are getting God's work done. We don't determine God's will by casting lots, but if we know the Scriptures and take time to pray, we can discover God's will.

The fact that Judas was in the disciple band indicates that no Christian group on earth is perfect, and the fact that Matthias is not famous indicates that not every servant is a Peter, a John, or a Paul. Let's give our best to the Lord and seek only to glorify Jesus Christ.

> Therefore, whether you eat or drink, or whatever you do, do all to the glory of God.
>
> 1 Corinthians 10:31

71

> Now *all who believed were together*, and had all
> things in common.

ACTS 2:44

Three times during our ministry years, the churches
have chosen us, but twice my wife and I were serving
in parachurch ministries and we had to choose the
church. No church is perfect, but you do want to find one
that is as close to the New Testament pattern as possible,
and Acts 2:40–47 is an excellent portrait of a Spirit-directed
church. We wanted a church that was *together* in the things
that really counted and not divided over matters that were
trivial. Jesus prayed that his followers would be one (John
17:11, 21–22), and the church described in Acts 2 certainly
qualifies. This church had "togetherness."

Believers should be together in *their faith in Jesus Christ*.
They must be "believers," which means putting personal faith
in Jesus as personal Savior and Lord and making it known
publicly. Before uniting with a church family, you must be born
again into the family of God where there are neither ethnic nor
gender qualifications nor political, economic, or social requirements, for true believers are "all one in Christ Jesus" (Gal. 3:28).
Christian doctrine is an essential part of Christian unity (Acts
2:42), and this is where the Bible comes in. At Pentecost, Peter
preached the Word of God and presented Jesus Christ in his
death, burial, and resurrection. Augustine said it perfectly: "In
essentials, unity; in nonessentials, liberty; in all things, charity."

Believers should be together in *their fear of the Lord* (v. 43).
In his sermon, Peter said, "Therefore let all the house of Israel
know assuredly that God has made this Jesus, whom you crucified, both Lord and Christ" (v. 36). Godly fear means giving
the Lord the respect and worship that he deserves, taking his

commandments seriously, and wanting to please him in all that we think, say, and do. Fearing the Lord means not deliberately disobeying God and thereby tempting him to chasten us. True worship honors the Lord and brings glory to his name. It is not religious entertainment or shallow excitement but lasting spiritual enrichment. Worship, prayer, the study of the Word, and sacrificial service are all a part of fearing and serving God.

Believers should be together *in fellowship in the Spirit*. Spiritual fellowship doesn't mean chatting and laughing over a cup of coffee and a pastry, although there is nothing wrong with that. In the New Testament, the word *fellowship* means "to have in common." The more we become like Jesus, the closer we become as Christians; the closer we get to one another, the more we can understand each other and sympathize and minister to one another. God tells us to love one another, pray for one another, forgive one another, encourage one another—the "one another" admonitions in the New Testament are many! The early church took into their fellowship the many converted visitors in Jerusalem in that Pentecostal season, people from many nations. Christian fellowship must be as encompassing as God's love for us (Eph. 3:19–21).

Believers should be together in *their faithful witness to the lost*. "And the Lord added to the church daily those who were being saved" (Acts 2:47). Not just once a week on Sunday, or once a year at the annual "revival," but daily! This means believers were giving their witness at the market, at work, in the neighborhood, and in the temple, by the way they lived and the words they spoke. They shared the gospel wherever they went, as the Holy Spirit enabled them (Acts 1:8), and the Lord gave the increase.

We would like to be a part of that kind of church, but maybe the Lord has to start with us!

> We, being many, are one body in Christ, and individually members of one another.
>
> Romans 12:5

72

Yet now, brethren, I know that *you did it in ignorance*, as did also your rulers.

ACTS 3:17

An old adage states, "Ignorance is no excuse in the sight of the law." If I drive too fast in a school zone, I can't excuse myself by telling the officer who stops me that I didn't know it was a school zone. It is impossible for legislators to enact laws geared to the knowledge and experience of every citizen. Yet Peter seems to be using the ignorance of the people in the temple as an excuse for the crucifixion of Jesus. He had just accused them of denying Jesus and asking for a murderer (Barabbas) to be set free. They killed their Messiah, the Prince of Life! Does that mean that their sin is forgiven because of their ignorance?

Peter knew that the Law of Moses provided sacrifices for unintentional sins but not for high-handed, deliberate sins against the Lord (Num. 15:27–31). For example, when people discovered they had accidently touched a dead animal and therefore were unclean, they could bring a sacrifice to the priests and be cleansed. But anyone who deliberately defied the Lord and broke the law was guilty and could be severely punished, even slain. The book of Hebrews mentions that, on the annual Day of Atonement, the high priest offered sacrifices for the forgiveness of sins he and the people had committed "in ignorance" (Heb. 9:6–7). God had mercy on those who, in their ignorance, had gone astray (5:1–3).

But the sacrifice of Jesus on the cross carries the matter even further, for he prayed, "Father, forgive them, for they do not know what they do" (Luke 23:34). The Jewish religious leaders sinned when they deliberately crucified Jesus; they closed their eyes to the flood of light God had given them to enable them to see clearly, but the crowds who agreed with them were ignorant of what was transpiring. The leaders had the Old Testament prophets to instruct them, but in their willful and selfish plotting they ignored the very Scriptures they read and esteemed. Jesus said that the Pharisees were blind men leading blind people (Matt. 15:14), yet the Pharisees thought their great knowledge of Scripture made them the true leaders. But Jesus said they understood neither the Scriptures nor the power of God (22:29). The finished work of Jesus on the cross has once and for all paid the price for all sin for all time, and you are forgiven all trespasses (Col. 2:13).

Let's consider the witness of Paul. "I was formerly a blasphemer, a persecutor, and an insolent man; but I obtained mercy because I did it ignorantly in unbelief" (1 Tim. 1:13). Paul thought he was serving the Lord by opposing the church. The prayer of Jesus as the soldiers nailed him to the cross was answered in the salvation of Paul. Ignorance of who Jesus is and what he accomplished will not automatically save anybody, but it does open the gates of mercy to people who do not know the way of salvation. Satan blinds the eyes of the lost so they don't understand the Scriptures or realize the greatness of the grace of God. He wants people to think they are hopeless and helpless because of their sins. But the promise still stands: "And it shall come to pass that whoever calls on the name of the LORD shall be saved" (Acts 2:21).

Some people are lost who do know about the cross because of their willful refusal to believe. Others are lost because nobody has yet told them the good news of the gospel. No child of God who has paid any attention to the Scriptures and hymnody can claim ignorance of the responsibility we have to bear witness to a lost world. Are we praying specifically for lost people? Do we ask the Lord for daily opportunities to share Christ?

> How then shall they call on Him in whom they have not believed? And how shall they believe in Him of whom they have not heard? And how shall they hear without a preacher?
>
> Romans 10:14

73

Nor is there salvation in any other, for *there is no other name* under heaven given among men by which we must be saved.

ACTS 4:12

Knowing the meaning of biblical names is often the key to understanding the people who bore them, and a change in names is often associated with a radical change in that person's life. Abram ("high father") became Abraham ("father of a multitude"); Simon ("hearing") became Peter ("rock"); and Saul ("asked of God") became Paul ("little"). The name the apostle Peter was exalting before the Jewish council was Jesus ("savior"), the name that is "above every name" (Phil. 2:9) and the name of the person we all need to trust.

There is no other name under heaven *if you want to go to heaven*. The angel told Joseph that Mary would bear a Son and they were to name him *Jesus*, "for He will save His people from their sins" (Matt. 1:20–21). Jesus means "savior," for "the Father has sent the Son as Savior of the world" (1 John 4:14). Some people want Jesus only as an example to follow or as a teacher to instruct them, but as helpful as teachers and examples are, our greatest need is for a savior. "Believe on the Lord Jesus Christ, and you will be saved" (Acts 16:31).

There is no other name under heaven *if you want your prayers answered*. Jesus said, "And whatever you ask in My name, that will I do, that the Father may be glorified in the Son. If you ask anything in My name, I will do it" (John 14:13–14). To ask in the name of Jesus means to ask what he would ask. "What would Jesus ask?" is a very important question, because it is only when we ask in his will that we can expect him to answer (1 John 5:14–15). We must spend time in the Word of God and find out what our Lord wants us to ask.

There is no other name under heaven *if you want to understand your Bible*. The theme of the Bible is Jesus Christ, the Son of God, the Savior of the world. The two men walking to Emmaus were privileged to hear Jesus teach the Old Testament Scriptures, and they had burning hearts as they listened (Luke 24:13–35). "He expounded to them in all the Scriptures the things concerning Himself" (v. 27). The Spirit is willing to do this for us!

There is no other name under heaven *if you want to be an effective witness*. Our witnessing must not focus on denominations or churches or preachers; it must point to Jesus (Acts 1:8). We must say with Peter, "For we cannot but speak the things which we have seen and heard" (4:20). That is witnessing, simply telling others what we have personally seen and heard regarding Jesus Christ, and backing up our words with our walk.

There is no other name under heaven *if you want to experience personal victory*. In his life, death, resurrection, and ascension, Jesus has defeated the world (John 16:33), the flesh (Rom. 6:1–7), and the devil (Col. 2:13–15). He has sent the Holy Spirit to dwell in every believer and he enables us to walk in newness of life. By faith we can say with Paul, "I can do all things through Christ who strengthens me" (Phil. 4:13).

There is no other name in heaven *if you want a living hope*. The Lord Jesus Christ *is* our hope (1 Tim. 1:1). When Jesus is our Lord, the future is our friend. No matter what reports we hear about the world situation and no matter what personal problems we may have, we still look up and expect the return of our Lord. Christian hope is not "hope so" but the assurance that the future is in his hands. We have a living Christ and therefore have a living hope (1 Pet. 1:3).

Finally, my brethren, be strong in the Lord and in the power of His might.

Ephesians 6:10

74

Then *the word of God spread*, and the number of the disciples multiplied greatly in Jerusalem, and a great many of the priests were obedient to the faith.

ACTS 6:7

Our text ends an account of how the church solved a serious problem and experienced a great harvest of souls. There was a division in the Jerusalem church, and division always weakens ministry. Also, some of the people were complaining, and that always robs a church of spiritual power. The real problem was that the apostles were so busy serving tables that they could not focus on prayer and the ministry of the Word (Acts 6:4). Once the apostles got their priorities straightened out and the church enlisted new workers, the blessing began to come. The Word of God is alive (Heb. 4:12; Ps. 119:50) and as people receive Christ, it spreads from person to person, but our sins too often block the way to blessings.

The Word of God is alive and active in creation, and we see the results from day to day and from season to season. "For He spoke, and it was done; He commanded, and it stood fast" (Ps. 33:9). "He sends out His command to the earth; His word runs very swiftly" (147:15). "Fire and hail, snow and clouds; stormy wind, [fulfill] His word" (148:8).

God's living Word must be active in each local church. As we sing the Word in worship and teach and preach the Word, its truth and life must go from us and grow within us. Each preacher, teacher, worship leader, and singer must be sure that the ministry is grounded in and bounded by the Word of God. "Let the word of Christ dwell in you richly in all wisdom, teaching and admonishing one another in psalms and hymns and spiritual songs, singing with grace in your

152

hearts to the Lord" (Col. 3:16). Pastors must not be so busy in lesser matters that they have no time for prayer and the Word of God. Once the apostles were relieved of serving tables, they had time for prayer and preaching, and God gave them a great ingathering of souls.

The Word must be alive in world evangelism. "Finally, brethren, pray for us, that the word of the Lord may run swiftly and be glorified, just as it is with you" (2 Thess. 3:1). Paul wrote to Timothy and reminded him that, though he himself was jailed and in chains, the Word of God was not in chains and could go from witness to witness and bear fruit (2 Tim. 2:9). All of us as believers must pray for and support those people and ministries that get the Word out to other nations and peoples where we ourselves cannot go. We can't support all of them, but we must do the best we can with what God gives us. The gospel can bear fruit anywhere in the world (Col. 1:6), if we work together to plow the soil, plant the seed, water the seed with our prayers, and are ready to reap the harvest (John 4:35–38; 1 Cor. 3:5–9).

But we must be sure that the living Word of God is active in our own personal lives. Let's follow the example of the believers in Thessalonica for whom Paul gave thanks. "For this reason we also thank God without ceasing, because when you received the word of God which you heard from us, you welcomed it not as the word of men, but as it is in truth, the word of God, which also effectively works in you who believe" (1 Thess. 2:13). The living Word that works in this world also works in us if we receive it, believe it, and obey it. As the truth grows in us, we grow and bear fruit for the glory of Jesus Christ.

May it be said of us and our ministries, "But the word of God grew and multiplied. . . . So the word of the Lord grew mightily and prevailed" (Acts 12:24; 19:20).

Grow in the grace and knowledge of our Lord and Savior Jesus Christ.

2 Peter 3:18

153

75

> While it remained, *was it not your own?* And after
> it was sold, was it not in your own control? Why
> have you conceived this thing in your heart? You
> have not lied to men but to God.

ACTS 5:4

Of course the property Ananias sold was his own! He could have kept it, given it away, or sold it, and when he sold it he could have used the money as he saw fit, so long as he used it lawfully. The problem was not one of *ownership* but of *stewardship*. Yes, money was involved, but the key issue was *motive*: what Ananias and Sapphira had in their hearts, not what they had in their hands. They thought they could deceive their fellow Christians and the Lord, but they were wrong.

It all began with *Barnabas the encourager*, which is what his name means (Acts 4:36). His home was in Cyprus and he probably was in Jerusalem to celebrate Pentecost. When and where he became a Christian and how he acquired his property, we do not know, but he certainly was an exemplary disciple of Jesus Christ. *Never underestimate the impact of one sacrificial act of Christian service.* His gift to the Lord certainly helped the new Christians being cared for by the church, some of whom were far from home; but at the same time, by sharing his gift he revealed the wickedness in the hearts of Ananias and Sapphira. That's what happened to Lot when Abraham offered to give him any piece of land he desired in Canaan. Lot's choice revealed the sin in his heart, because he chose to live near the wicked city of Sodom (Gen. 13). When Mary of Bethany anointed Jesus with the expensive ointment, it revealed the covetousness in the heart of Judas (John 12:1–8). We may think our service accomplishes very

154

little, and we may be criticized by others, but one day we will discover in heaven all God did with our ministry.

Enter *Ananias and Sapphira, the pretenders*. There are a number of sins involved in this episode, and one sin led to another. Peter knew that Ananias had "conceived" this plot with Satan's help (Acts 5:4), as a child is conceived in the mother's womb and grows (James 1:13–15). Their scheme probably started with envy. When they saw what Barnabas did, they decided they wanted the same reputation he had gained. *They wanted to make people think they were more spiritual than they really were, but they would not pay the price*. Envy led to pride, pride led to hypocrisy, and hypocrisy was strengthened by lies. They lied to the church, to Peter, to the Holy Spirit, and to themselves. They really thought they could get away with their scheme, but they were serving Satan, not the Lord, and Satan is a liar and a murderer (John 8:44). The fact that the husband and wife had plotted this masquerade together makes their sin even more evil.

Peter, the spiritual leader, knew what was going on, and he exposed the hypocrisy of the couple. The Lord arranged it so that Peter spoke to them individually, Ananias first and then Sapphira. Peter made it clear to Ananias that the property was his and the money was his and that there was no need to lie about it. God struck Ananias and he died instantly. Then Sapphira came in, not knowing that her husband was dead and buried. Satan always keeps his servants in the dark, while the Father keeps his obedient children informed (John 15:15). Judas the betrayer comes to mind. Satan had entered Ananias and Sapphira just as he had entered Judas (13:27); and when Judas went out from the upper room, "it was night" (v. 30).

To lie to one another is to lie to God, and to lie to God is to invite either chastening or judgment, for God wants his people to "walk in truth" (3 John 4). It is a dangerous thing to lie to the Holy Spirit, for the Holy Spirit is the Spirit of truth (John 16:13).

I have no greater joy than to hear that my children walk in truth.

3 John 4

155

76

> As [Paul] journeyed, he came near Damascus, *and suddenly a light shone* around him from heaven.
>
> ACTS 9:3

Light and darkness are frequently found in the Bible, the light symbolizing God, holiness, life, and truth, while the darkness picturing Satan, sin, lies, and death. Jesus is the light of the world (John 8:12) and Christians are lights in the world (Phil. 2:15). Heaven is a city of light (Rev. 22:5), while hell is "outer darkness" (Matt. 8:12). In his life and ministry, the apostle Paul illustrates the special relationship believers have with the light.

Opposing the light. Saul of Tarsus, who became Paul the apostle, was born into a strict Jewish home and studied in Jerusalem under the esteemed rabbi Gamaliel. He considered himself blameless before God's law (Phil. 3:6), and he devoted himself to persecuting Christians. He arrested them, punished them, and even consented to killing them (Acts 7:57–8:3; 26:9–11). Convinced that Moses was right and Jesus was wrong and dead, Saul of Tarsus sought to destroy the light.

Seeing the light. Paul's conversion experience is recorded in Acts 9 by Dr. Luke and spoken of by Paul himself in Acts 22:1–21 and 26:1–23. In all three accounts you find reference to the light. As Paul was traveling to Damascus, "suddenly a light shone around him from heaven" (Acts 9:3). Paul told the Jews in the temple that "suddenly a great light from heaven shone around me" (22:6). In his witness before King Agrippa, Paul said, "I saw a light from heaven, brighter than the sun, shining around me" (26:13). We go from "a light," to "a great light," to "a light from heaven, brighter than the sun." "But the path of the just is like the shining sun, that shines ever brighter unto the perfect day" (Prov. 4:18). Historically, the light itself does not change, but Paul's descriptions illustrate how the light becomes brighter to us as we obey Christ.

Sharing the light. God called Paul to be a witness of Jesus Christ to the Gentiles. Paul describes these people in Romans 1:18–32. In his commission to Paul and his team, the Lord gave them Isaiah 49:6 as a key verse: "I will also give You as a light to the Gentiles, that You should be My salvation to the ends of the earth" (*see* Acts 13:47). Jesus told Paul that he sent him to the Gentiles "to open their eyes in order to turn them from darkness to light, and from the power of Satan to God, that they may receive forgiveness of sins" (Acts 26:18). The church today has that commission, to take the gospel to every tribe and nation, to "proclaim the praises of Him who called you out of darkness into His marvelous light" (1 Pet. 2:9). Paul was faithful to that calling and endured much suffering and persecution to accomplish the task. Are we that faithful today?

Entering the light. For the spiritually blind unbelievers, life only becomes darker and darker. The more they resist the light, the blinder they become, because Satan, "the god of this age," has blinded them to God's truth (2 Cor. 4:4). But as we saw in Proverbs 4:18, the Christian believer lives in a light that gets brighter and brighter! We are not heading for a sunset, for if we should die before Jesus returns, we will move into a city of light where night will never come. It will be glorious! As he sat in a Roman cell, Paul looked forward to going to glory. He wrote to Timothy, "I know whom I have believed and am persuaded that He is able to keep what I have committed to Him until that Day" (2 Tim. 1:12). He was ready to die, knowing that a crown awaited him in heaven (4:7–8). Death for believers is not sunset but sunrise!

Have you seen the light? Are you sharing the light with others?

In Him was life, and the life was the light of men. And the light shines in the darkness, and the darkness did not comprehend it.

John 1:4–5

77

The word which God sent to the children of Israel, preaching peace through Jesus Christ—*He is Lord of all.*

ACTS 10:36

As Christians, we must faithfully learn spiritual truth and translate that learning into living, because what we believe determines how we behave. Peter's last words in his second letter make this clear: "but grow in the grace and knowledge of our Lord and Savior Jesus Christ" (2 Pet. 3:18). Jesus had given Peter the keys of the kingdom (Matt. 16:19) and he had opened the door of faith to the Jews and to the Samaritans (Acts 2; 8). Now the time had come for him to open the door to the Gentiles, a radical step for an orthodox Jew. God prepared Peter for this ministry and also prepared the Gentiles who would receive his ministry.

Peter learned from a vision (10:9–16). About noon, while Peter was waiting for a meal to be prepared, God took advantage of his hunger and showed him all kinds of animals, reptiles, and birds, and commanded him, "Rise, Peter; kill and eat." Peter's response shocks us: "Not so, Lord! For I have never eaten anything common or unclean" (v. 14). Peter had kept a kosher home all the years after his conversion and had obeyed the Mosaic dietary laws, even though Jesus had taught the disciples that all foods are clean (Mark 7:14–23). He had also told them that he had "other sheep" (the Gentiles) that he would bring into the fold (John 10:16). The vision and the voice were repeated three times, but Peter was so rigid in his convictions that he refused to obey Jesus after calling him "Lord." We can say "No" or we can say "Lord," but we cannot say "No, Lord." In this vision, God showed Peter that

Gentiles are not unclean before God and that Gentiles did not have to become Jews before they could become Christians.

Peter learned from a visit (Acts 10:17–48). The Lord introduced Peter to a Gentile community, and Peter got the message: "God has shown me that I should not call any man common or unclean" (v. 28). God didn't tell the Gentiles to "climb higher" and become Jews. He told the Jews they were sinners just like the Gentiles! "For all have sinned and fall short of the glory of God" (Rom. 3:23). God is no respecter of persons (Deut. 10:17; 1 Pet. 1:17). So ready was this congregation to hear God's word that Peter never got to finish his sermon! When he said, "To [Jesus] all the prophets witness that, through His name, whoever believes in Him will receive remission of sins" (Acts 10:43), *the people believed and were saved.* End of sermon!

What we can learn from Peter. A gracious Lord, a praying soldier, a prepared congregation, and a prepared preacher— and the whole congregation was converted. Jesus is Lord of all! At first Peter hesitated to visit a Gentile home, but God removed his prejudices and showed him what he could do if only his servant would obey. Jesus is "Lord of all" and is "not willing that any should perish but that all should come to repentance" (2 Pet. 3:9). The Holy Spirit came upon each new believer in the house of Cornelius and moved them to praise God for what he had done. Because of the work of Jesus on the cross, the wall that stood between Jews and Gentiles had been broken down and the old covenant law had been removed (Eph. 2:14–15). Because of Peter's obedience to God's will, the door was now open for Paul to become the apostle to the Gentiles.

Why didn't the Lord have Peter take the gospel to the Gentiles sooner? Because he has his times and seasons and works according to his perfect plan. Jesus is Lord of all heaven and earth and we are his servants. We must say, "Yes, Lord" and do the Master's will.

> There is neither Jew nor Gentile, neither slave nor free, neither male nor female, for you are all one in Christ Jesus.
>
> Galatians 3:28 TNIV

78

> You know . . . in what manner I always lived
> among you, serving the Lord with all humility,
> *with many tears and trials* which happened to me
> by the plotting of the Jews.

ACTS 20:18–19

Every devoted Christian who is seeking to serve and glorify the Lord knows the meaning of "many tears and trials." One of the first questions the new believer asks is, "Why am I experiencing so much trouble?" But the Lord told us this would happen (John 15:18–16:4), and so did Paul (Acts 14:22; 1 Thess. 3:1) and Peter (1 Pet. 3:18–4:19). But why *do* we suffer?

We have an evil enemy opposing us. "Be sober, be vigilant; because your adversary the devil walks about like a roaring lion, seeking whom he may devour" (1 Pet. 5:8). "But I fear, lest somehow, as the serpent deceived Eve by his craftiness, so your minds may be corrupted from the simplicity that is in Christ" (2 Cor. 11:3). Satan devours, deceives, and destroys, and we must be alert. But the grace of God can turn Satan's weapons into tools that build us up (12:7–10). Start each day by putting on the armor of God by faith (Eph. 6:10–18), and use the sword of the Spirit to refute Satan's lies and the shield of faith to extinguish his fiery darts.

We have a hostile world against us. "In the world you will have tribulation; but be of good cheer, I have overcome the world" (John 16:33). Satan uses the world system to entice and corrupt us, but the lost people in the world are the "fish" the Lord wants us to "catch" in the gospel net (Matt. 4:18–22). Jesus wept over the people in Jerusalem because they refused to receive him (Luke 19:41), and Paul also wept over his Jewish kinsmen (Rom. 9:1–3). Sometimes we suffer that we might be a testimony to the lost. Paul and Silas were illegally humiliated, beaten, and jailed in Philippi, yet God used them to bring salvation to the jailer and his family (Acts 16:16–34). Paul wept because the world had gotten into the church and was causing trouble (Phil. 3:18; 2 Cor. 2:4), and so we should weep and pray today (Ps. 119:136).

We have a spiritual potential within us. It was suffering that helped bring out the leadership skills in Joseph, David, Peter, and Paul. Our Father wants us to be "conformed to the image of His Son" (Rom. 8:29), and part of that curriculum includes "the fellowship of His sufferings" (Phil. 3:10). We should "glory in tribulations, knowing that tribulation produces perseverance; and perseverance, character; and character, hope" (Rom. 5:3–4). The potter molds the vessel and puts it into the furnace where it is hardened. Claim Ephesians 2:10 and Philippians 2:12.

We have a heavenly glory before us. "For I consider that the sufferings of this present time are not worthy to be compared with the glory which shall be revealed in us" (Rom. 8:18). God keeps a record of our tears and, if we are faithful, one day will reward us accordingly (Ps. 56:8). "Weeping may endure for a night, but joy comes in the morning" (Ps. 30:5). Even our Lord had to endure suffering before he could enter into his glory (Luke 24:25–27). Our joyful endurance is itself a witness to the lost and an investment in future glory (1 Pet. 4:12–13). Even if you are weeping, keep sowing the seeds of truth and love and you will reap a harvest of rejoicing (Ps. 126:5–6). One day in heaven we will meet the people who trusted Christ because we witnessed and prayed (1 Thess. 2:19–20), and what a time of rejoicing that will be!

Tears and trials are important elements in faithful Christian living, so let's "run with endurance the race that is set before us" (Heb. 12:1). The best is yet to come.

> We are His workmanship, created in Christ Jesus for good works, which God prepared beforehand that we should walk in them.
>
> Ephesians 2:10

79

> *I commend you to God* and to *the word of His grace*, which is able to build you up and give you an inheritance among all those who are sanctified.

The apostle Paul was saying goodbye to the elders of the church of Ephesus, many of whom he no doubt personally led to faith in Christ. God's servants come and go in our lives, and though we love them and benefit from their varied ministries, we dare not idolize them. We must build on eternal and unchanging essentials to enjoy a satisfying and consistent Christian life.

The unchanging God. "For I am the LORD, I do not change" (Mal. 3:6). "Jesus Christ is the same yesterday, today, and forever" (Heb. 13:8). Imagine what it would be like to have a man the caliber of Paul as your pastor! He had seen Jesus in his glory and heard him speak, and he had even been in heaven and returned. He had a gift of healing, he was a faithful man of prayer, and he knew the deep things of God. But as great as Paul was in spiritual matters, if he saw you building your life on him, he would have said, "Build your life on Jesus Christ! He is the foundation!" "For no other foundation can anyone lay than that which is laid, which is Jesus Christ" (1 Cor. 3:11). It's tragic when unspiritual people turn their "favorite" preacher, teacher, or writer into a religious celebrity, the way the believers did in the Corinthian church (1:10–17). It's also unfortunate that some Christian workers encourage this kind of unbiblical behavior and bask in it. They need to imitate what Peter said when Cornelius fell at his feet: "Stand up; I myself am also a man" (Acts 10:26).

The unchanging Word of God. "Forever, O LORD, Your word is settled in heaven" (Ps. 119:89). "Heaven and earth

162

will pass away, but My words will by no means pass away" (Matt. 24:35). It is the Bible that reveals to us the character, works, and purposes of the one true and living God, and we must test whatever religious leaders say by that unchanging Word. From time to time we have new translations of the Bible, not because the Bible changes but because language changes. *God wants us to understand who he is and what he wants us to be and to do.* Nobody understands everything in Scripture and there is always more to learn. Those Ephesian elders did not have complete Bibles as we have today. Old Testament scrolls were available but expensive, and the New Testament was still being written, yet the early believers had enough of God's Word to know the basics and put them into practice. And don't see your Bible as a book of laws and rules but as "the word of His grace" (Acts 20:32), for his grace is revealed in the Bible from beginning to end.

The unchanging grace of God. Grace is God's favor given freely to undeserving people like us. The message of salvation is "the gospel of the grace of God" (Acts 20:24), and there is no other saving message from God. The gospel is that "Christ died for our sins according to the Scriptures, and that He was buried, and that He rose again the third day according to the Scriptures" (1 Cor. 15:3–4). Jesus died in our place! This is the grace of God. "And it shall come to pass that whoever calls on the name of the Lord shall be saved" (Acts 2:21). But God's grace not only saves us, it also meets our every need; for he says, "My grace is sufficient for you" (2 Cor. 12:9). The treasury of God's grace is available to every believer (Rom. 5:1–2). God's throne is a throne of grace for us, not a throne of judgment (Heb. 4:14–16); and it is available to us at all times and for all needs. The supply is limitless and "He gives more grace" (James 4:6).

> So I say to you, ask, and it will be given to you; seek, and you will find; knock, and it will be opened to you.
>
> Luke 11:9

80

> Among whom you also are *the called of Jesus Christ*.
>
> ROMANS 1:6

Peter made it clear that "whoever calls on the name of the LORD shall be saved" (Acts 2:21); but before we call upon God, he first calls us! After Adam and Eve sinned, God came to the garden and called, "Where are you?" (Gen. 3:9). "My sheep hear My voice, and I know them, and they follow Me" (John 10:27). This is why the apostle Paul identified saved people as "the called of Jesus Christ." But what does this calling involve?

We are called to belong. In some versions, our text reads "called to belong to Jesus Christ," and this is a valid translation. Why would Jesus want sinners like us to be his friends (15:15), his sheep (10:27–29), and his servants (Rom. 1:1)? Only because of his great love for us. Before we trusted Christ, we were hopelessly enslaved by the world, the flesh, and the devil (Eph. 2:1–3), but he set us free and claimed us as his own; and we gladly own him as our Master. As Norman B. Clayton wrote in one of his songs, "Now I belong to Jesus / Jesus belongs to me / Not for the years of time alone / But for eternity." Because we belong to Jesus, we also belong to one another as members of his body (5:30). You cannot belong to the Bridegroom and ignore the bride. As God's people, we belong to each other and we need each other.

We are called to behave. We are saints (Rom. 1:7). The word means "set apart ones" and refers to all believers, not just to a spiritual elite. All true believers are saints right now. Local churches are made up of saints (1 Cor. 14:33). We have been delivered from the world, the flesh, and the devil. We have been brought into God's kingdom and have the Holy Spirit dwelling within us, and so we are able to live as "overcomers" and glorify God by our obedience. This means doing what is "fitting for saints" (Eph. 5:3). God's saints are not sinless, but they do sin less and less and less as they grow in the Lord. "Therefore, if anyone is in Christ, he is a new creation; old things have passed away; behold, all things have become new" (2 Cor. 5:17). Let's live like saints!

We are called to love and be loved. The saints in Rome were "beloved of God" (Rom. 1:7), but so are the saints in Chicago, London, Nairobi, and wherever you live. In Matthew, Mark, and Luke, the word *beloved* is used nine times and always applies to Jesus, the beloved Son of God. But Romans 1:7 applies it to *all* the saints—"beloved of God." The Father has "made us accepted in the Beloved" (Eph. 1:6). "My beloved is mine, and I am his" (Song of Sol. 2:16; 6:3). Our love for each other constrains us to obey him and to serve (1 Cor. 4:14). This love also motivates us to spend time in his Word, in prayer, and in fellowship with him and his people. If we truly love Jesus, we will love the saints who make up his church.

We are called to become. I like what Jesus said to Simon the first time he met him: "You are Simon the son of Jonah. You shall be called Cephas" (John 1:41–42). *Cephas* is Aramaic and means "a stone," which in Greek is *Peter.* "You are—you shall be!" That is the Christian life. In Jesus Christ, we have the "right [authority] to become." (John 1:12). To become what? Whatever the Lord has planned for us to be. Moses and Jeremiah both argued with God that they were not leadership material, but God transformed them and made them effective leaders. One day every true believer will become just like Jesus, "for we shall see Him as He is" (1 John 3:1–3).

What greater privilege is there on earth than being "the called of Jesus Christ"?

> But as many as received Him, to them He gave the right to become children of God, to those who believe in His name.
>
> John 1:12

81

And not only that, but *we also glory in tribulations*,
knowing that tribulation produces perseverance.

ROMANS 5:3

There are times when the pressures and pains of life make
us feel like quitting and finding a place to hide, except
for one thing: we are Christians and Christians don't
quit. The word in our text translated *glory* means "to exult, to
rejoice triumphantly," and that is exactly what the Lord enables
us to do in times of trouble if we put our trust in him. "Our
light affliction, which is but for a moment, is working for us a
far more exceeding and eternal weight of glory" (2 Cor. 4:17).
No matter how we feel, faith is still the victory.

Faith transforms tribulation into assurance. In the parable of
the sower (Matt. 13:1–9, 18–23), the seed is the Word of God
and the soils represent the human heart and show how different
people respond to the Word. Some hearts are hard and never
receive the seed. Some hearts are shallow and the seed cannot
take root. The sun represents tribulations. The rootless plant
has no way to secure water, so it withers and dies. Plants need
sunlight and Christians need trials, but only the true believer
with a spiritual "root system" can draw upon the resources
of God's grace and not wither and die. At some point, early
in the Christian life, the Lord permits us to experience trials
so that we can know for sure we belong to his family. To have
that assurance is worth going through the trials.

Faith transforms tribulation into a tool. Satan wants to use
trials as weapons to destroy us, but God uses these trials to
form us into the vessels he wants us to be. Our afflictions will
work *for us* and not *against* us as we claim God's promises and
submit to him. "My brethren, count it all joy when you fall into
various trials, knowing that the testing of your faith produces

patience. But let patience have its perfect work, that you may be perfect and complete, lacking nothing" (James 1:2–4). God used trials to mature Joseph and David and turn them into effective leaders, and he can do the same for us. Our English word "tribulation" comes from the Latin word *tribulum*, the name the Romans gave to the spiked wooden planks the oxen pulled over the sheaves to separate the grain and cut the straw. God wants us to produce a great harvest for his glory.

Faith transforms tribulation into eternal glory. "We walk by faith, not by sight" (2 Cor. 5:7). When Christ's glory is revealed we will be glad with exceeding joy (1 Pet. 4:13). "Blessed are you when they revile and persecute you, and say all kinds of evil against you falsely for My sake," Jesus said. "Rejoice and be exceedingly glad, for great is your reward in heaven" (Matt. 5:11–12). Faith and patience in tribulation are investments today that will pay great dividends in eternity. The believer who triumphs over trials will receive the crown of life (James 1:12).

Faith transforms tribulation into testimony. We live before a watching world and the way we respond to disappointment, trials, and conflicts gives us opportunities to bear witness to the lost people who know us. "Yet if anyone suffers as a Christian, let him not be ashamed, but let him glorify God in this matter" (1 Pet. 4:16). When we rejoice instead of complain and worship instead of whine, the unsaved take notice and wonder how it can happen. Paul and Silas were illegally put into prison in Philippi, but they prayed and sang praises and God gave them the privilege of leading the jailer and his family to faith in Christ (Acts 16:16–34).

The cross is the greatest evidence that suffering in the will of God leads to glory. Jesus leads the way! Let's follow him by faith and watch him turn trials into triumphs.

> Then Jesus said to His disciples, "If anyone desires to come after Me, let him deny himself, and take up his cross, and follow Me."
>
> Matthew 16:24

82

Therefore, brethren, we are debtors—not to the flesh, to live according to the flesh.

ROMANS 8:12

A familiar hymn says "Jesus paid it all, / All to him I owe," and those words are true, but let's not forget the debt we owe to the Holy Spirit. Consider some of the titles of the Spirit and you will see how much debt we are in.

He is *the Spirit of Christ* (Rom. 8:9). In the conception and birth of Christ (Luke 1:35) as well as in his atoning sacrifice (Heb. 9:14) and resurrection (Rom. 1:4), the Holy Spirit was at work. Jesus taught and preached, healed and raised the dead, and helped the poor and needy all in the Spirit's power (Luke 4:17–19). The Spirit who dwells within us longs to make us more like Jesus so he can use us to glorify the Son of God.

He is *the Spirit of truth* (John 14:17; 15:26; 16:12–15). We would have no Bible were it not for the Holy Spirit, nor would we be able to understand the Bible. The Scriptures are inspired by the Spirit (2 Tim. 3:16–17) and were written by holy men of God "as they were moved by the Holy Spirit" (2 Pet. 1:20–21). The Spirit does use human pastors and teachers to minister the Word to his church (Eph. 4:11–12), but the Spirit also wants to teach us each time we read the Scriptures and meditate on them. When I was a lad in Sunday school, our superintendent often opened the session by having us sing "More About Jesus." Over the years, I have recalled the lines "Spirit of God, my teacher be, / Showing the things of Christ to me." When the Holy Spirit is in control, it's exciting to read and study the Bible.

He is *the Spirit of power* (Acts 1:8). We considered this text in meditation #69, so you might want to review it, but also consider Luke 4:14. After Jesus defeated Satan in the wilderness, he "returned in the power of the Spirit to Galilee." He read Isaiah 61:1–2 publicly in the synagogue *and applied every word to himself.* Jesus willingly yielded himself to the Spirit of God who enabled him to minister. The apostles also depended on the Spirit's power. "Or why look so intently on us, as though by our own power or godliness we had made this man walk?" Peter asked the temple crowd (Acts 3:12). Peter and John were indebted to the Holy Spirit for that miracle of healing, just as we today are indebted to him for any work we do that glorifies Christ.

He is *the Spirit of adoption* (Rom. 8:15). We do not enter God's family by adoption but by the new birth (1 Pet. 1:23), for we are "partakers of the divine nature" (2 Pet. 1:4). Adopted children do not have the same DNA as their new parents, but we share God's nature. We also have an adult standing in his family. The word translated *adoption* in Romans 8:15 means "to place as an adult son." *Our Father treats us as adults and not as children.* From the moment we enter his family, we can speak (pray) and we can understand what our Father is saying to us. No baby can do that. We are given access to the family riches (Rom. 5:2; Phil. 4:19), but no human baby can inherit. We can walk. We can feed ourselves. We know who our Father is and what he can do for us. Our adult standing makes it possible for us to grow in the Lord and serve him. Adoption is a marvelous blessing!

Now, do you feel indebted to the Holy Spirit? Do you depend on him? Do you thank him when he enables you to obey God, overcome temptation, and serve others? The familiar Doxology we sing tells us to "praise Father, Son, and Holy Ghost."

After all, we are debtors.

> Offer to God thanksgiving,
> And pay your vows to the Most High.
>
> Psalm 50:14

83

Therefore *judge nothing before the time*, until the Lord comes, who will both bring to light the hidden things of darkness and reveal the counsels of the hearts. Then each one's praise will come from God.

1 CORINTHIANS 4:5

To escape criticism," wrote American humorist Elbert Hubbard, "do nothing, say nothing, and be nothing." But Paul had work to do and wasn't willing to make that kind of foolish sacrifice. He knew the church at Corinth very well, its debates and divisions (1 Cor. 1:10–17) and its carnality (3:1–4), and he was prepared to face the enemy and solve the problems. Some personal offenses can simply be turned over to the Lord and forgotten. "Hatred stirs up strife, but love covers all sins" (Prov. 10:12; 1 Pet. 4:8). For Paul, it was a painful experience, but out of it we can learn how to behave like Christians when criticism comes our way.

When others judge us, let's remain calm and look to the Lord for the grace we need. Not all criticism is destructive. "Faithful are the wounds of a friend, but the kisses of an enemy are deceitful" (Prov. 27:6). If our critics are wrong, we can help them; if they are right, they have helped us. Honest criticism encourages us to examine our own hearts and seek the Lord's help, because we don't know our own hearts as we should (Jer. 17:9). We must also consider the source of the criticism, because there are people who inflate their own weak egos by finding fault with everybody else. Pray for them and go on and do your work. The Lord sometimes sends "sandpaper people" into our lives to give us some polish. Paul knew he was in God's will and wanted the best for the church at Corinth.

When we judge other people, we must be sure our motives are right, because there is a difference between honest evaluation and negative faultfinding. We are to speak the truth in love (Eph. 4:15) and base what we say on spiritual discernment and not personal prejudice. Paul prayed that the believers in Philippi would have spiritual discernment (Phil. 1:9–10) and commanded the believers at Thessalonica to "test all things; hold fast what is good" (1 Thess. 5:21). Mature Christians are those who "have their senses exercised to discern both good and evil" (Heb. 5:14). I have found it helpful to ask the Lord to arrange the meeting, where and when he wants me to speak to the person. To deal with sensitive matters in the wrong place, at the wrong time, and in the wrong attitude only makes matters worse. He has always guided me.

When the Lord returns, he will judge our works (1 Cor. 3:13) *and our motives* (4:5) *and reward us.* Paul mentions the judgment seat of Christ in Romans 14:10 and 2 Corinthians 5:10. We will not face our sins, for they have been judged at the cross and are forgotten (Heb. 8:12), but our sins affect our works, and our works shall be judged. However, the purpose of the judgment seat of Christ is to give rewards for faithful service. The Greek word translated "judgment seat" was used in the ancient Olympics for the place where the judges awarded prizes to the contestants. Our text indicates that "each one's praise will come from God." The Lord in his grace will find something to reward in each believer, whether great or small, and he will make no mistakes. Let's not seek praise and rewards from others, but only from the Lord. Human praise is soon forgotten, but God's rewards will be laid at the feet of Jesus for his eternal glory (Rev. 4:4, 10–11).

> You are worthy, O Lord,
> To receive glory and honor and power;
> For You created all things,
> And by Your will they exist and were created.
>
> Revelation 4:11

84

Therefore *let us keep the feast*, not with old leaven, nor with the leaven of malice and wickedness, but with the unleavened bread of sincerity and truth.

1 CORINTHIANS 5:8

The feast Paul wrote about is the Jewish Feast of Unleavened Bread. It immediately followed Passover and lasted for a week (Lev. 23:4–8). Before the feast, every bit of yeast had to be removed from the homes, and during the week no yeast could be used at all. The church doesn't observe this feast, but the metaphor of the feast has a message for us today and offers every Christian three opportunities.

To begin with, the metaphor gives us an opportunity for *taking in*. The Christian life is like a banquet, which means it is something we should enjoy. Too many professed Christians don't look like happy guests at a banquet; they look and act more like solemn pallbearers drafted for a funeral. But a banquet provides good food, fellowship with friends, the possibility of meeting new friends, and a happy time together *at no expense to us*. When you read the four Gospels, you can't help but be impressed with the number of times Jesus is described at the table enjoying a meal. Note also the number of parables that involve food. The future Jewish kingdom is described as a feast (Isa. 25:6–8; Ps. 22:25–29). The Lord can provide a feast for us even when we are "in the presence of [our] enemies" (Ps. 23:5). After starving in the far country, the prodigal son came home to a family feast (Luke 15:11–24), even though his proud older brother tried to make the occasion a family feud. Tears may be our diet on some days, but there will still be joy in our heart (Ps. 42:3; 80:5; Isa. 30:20). Look upon each day as another "course" in the feast the Father has spread for you and you will experience enjoyment and enrichment.

A second opportunity is the opportunity for *cleaning up*. To the people of Israel, yeast was a symbol of evil. Like sin, yeast seems a small thing, and yet when placed in the dough, it grows and puffs up the dough. Remember, Paul was writing to the "puffed up" Corinthians who refused to deal with sin in the church (1 Cor. 4:6, 18–19; 5:2; 13:4). Paul admonished them to get rid of "the old leaven" left over from their old life as well as "the leaven of malice and wickedness." Jesus warned his disciples against the leaven of the Pharisees, which was hypocrisy (Luke 12:1), as well as the teachings of the Pharisees and Sadducees (Matt. 16:6, 12). False doctrine is like yeast. It spreads quickly and quietly and before long infects an entire church (Gal. 5:7–9). A critic told evangelist Billy Sunday, "I don't believe in these revivals because they don't last." Billy Sunday replied, "Neither does a bath, but it's good to have one occasionally." Is there yeast in our lives that needs to be dealt with? Are we puffed up over it?

There is also the opportunity for *bringing in*. Unsaved people are not enjoying a feast. They are dead in sin and living on substitutes (Eph. 2:1–3), which means they are at a funeral and enduring a famine. The prodigal said, "I perish with hunger" (Luke 15:17), as must everyone who has never trusted Christ. It's our privilege to invite them to the banquet. Some believers are afraid to witness, but think of what we are offering: an invitation to salvation's supper from the Lord himself. "Come, for all things are now ready!" (14:17). "Why do you spend money for what is not bread, and your wage for what does not satisfy?" (Isa. 55:2). Dinner is served!

> He brought me to the banqueting house,
> and his banner over me was love.
>
> Song of Solomon 2:4

85

For we know in part and we prophesy in part.

First Corinthians 13 was not written to be read at weddings or funerals but at church business meetings and committee meetings. The church in Corinth was divided four ways and was defiled by the open sins of some of the members, yet the church boasted of having great spiritual knowledge. The phrase "we know in part" must have offended the church deeply, even though "we" included the apostle Paul, who certainly knew God and his Word. There are three healthy responses to those five words that will help edify us individually and unify us collectively.

First of all, the phrase should *humble us.* I have been studying the Bible since 1944 and have published commentaries on every book of the Bible, yet I would hesitate to say that I know the Bible. The more I study, the more I discover what I don't know. Historian Will Durant wrote, "Education is a progressive discovery of our own ignorance," and this is especially true of Bible study. King David wrote part of the Bible and yet confessed his own ignorance of Scripture (Ps. 40:5; 139:17–18), and Paul asked, "For who has known the mind of the LORD? Or who has become his counselor?" (Rom. 11:34). In 1 Corinthians 1–3, Paul uses the word *wisdom* seventeen times and contrasts God's wisdom with the world's wisdom. Corinth was known for its philosophers and teachers, and their spirit of controversy and pride had invaded the church, for "knowledge puffs up" (1 Cor. 8:1). True students of the Bible humble themselves and feel unworthy of the privilege of studying God's thoughts and deeds.

The phrase "For we know in part" also ought to *caution us.* In the inspired and inerrant Scriptures, God has given us all we

174

need for salvation, godliness, and service. Believers who give themselves to the Lord and his truth can become "thoroughly equipped for every good work" (2 Tim. 3:17). But we must be careful not to "systematize" Scripture so much that we think we have everything under control. "For we know in part," and if we don't have all the parts, we are handicapped. Newtonian physics was at one time the acme of scientific thought—and then Einstein came along. I am not saying we cannot trust the Bible, but only that we can't always trust every interpretation and explanation. The basics, I think, are clear, so that any sinner can understand and be saved and every believer can grow in grace and serve the Lord; beyond that, we must be humbly cautious. There is yet much for us to learn.

Finally, "For we know in part" should *encourage us*. Paul tells us that the day will come when we shall know just as fully as God knows us (1 Cor. 13:12). This doesn't mean that we will be as intelligent as God; it means that we will be in the perfect environment of heaven, in glorified bodies, learning what we either could not or did not learn on earth. During the coming ages in heaven there will be growth in our knowledge of God and the Scriptures. Today, the holy angels are learning by watching the church (1 Cor. 4:9; Eph. 3:10; 1 Pet. 1:12), and for all eternity God's people will be learning more and more about the things of the Lord. I believe the great acts of God will be explained to us, including what he did for us personally here on earth. We will also learn how the acts of God and our own actions have been brought together to accomplish his will. Let's start learning now!

Today, we are studying truth as though we were looking in a foggy mirror, but in heaven it will be "face to face." Let's prepare by learning as much of the Bible now as we can!

> Your hands have made me and fashioned me;
> Give me understanding, that I may learn Your
> commandments.
>
> Psalm 119:73

86

> Now thanks be to God who *always leads us in triumph* in Christ, and through us diffuses the fragrance of His knowledge in every place.
>
> 2 CORINTHIANS 2:14

All of us would enjoy life more if events always moved smoothly and on schedule, but life isn't organized that way. We encounter situations like canceled planes, sudden illnesses or injuries, car trouble, and unexpected visitors, and we just have to make the best of it. Paul had his share of trouble as he was traveling and ministering, and at one point he even wondered if he would come out of it alive (2 Cor. 1:8–11), but the Lord saw him through. Christian life and service involve burdens and battles, disappointments and dangers, and every believer must learn how to face reality and deal with it. Three familiar words help point the way to success.

Conflict. The first rule is "Expect it." The Lord and Satan have been in conflict ever since Lucifer rebelled and was cast out of heaven with his army of fallen angels (Isa. 14:12–15). Satan attacks God by attacking God's people. He tempted Eve, he attacked Job, he created problems for Israel, he tempted Jesus in the wilderness, he led Judas into treachery, he assaulted Paul, and he will continue to attack God's people until he is finally judged and cast into the lake of fire. His demonic assistants do their share of damage and our only sure defense is wearing the armor and using the sword and shield (Eph. 6:10–20). Satan can even work through believers (Matt. 16:21–23), so we must be on guard. God hasn't deserted you when the enemy starts attacking you. It's just the opposite! The presence of trouble may mean that the life you live and the work you do are interfering with Satan's insidious plans and he wants to silence you.

Conquest. "And who is sufficient for these things?" asks Paul (2 Cor. 2:16), and he answers in our text! The word *triumph* is significant and the church in Corinth knew exactly what Paul was referring to: the famous "Roman triumph," the greatest of parades in human history. When a Roman commander-in-chief won a singular victory on foreign soil, he was welcomed home with a "Roman triumph" parade. The requirements were that at least five thousand enemy soldiers were slain, many enemy officers were captured, valuable spoils were brought home, and new territory was gained for Rome. The hero rode at the head of the parade in a golden chariot followed by his officers, some of whom carried trophies of battle. The Roman priests were in the parade, burning incense to their gods, and at the end of the parade were the enemy captives who would entertain the citizens by fighting the lions in the stadium. Paul saw in this an illustration of Christ's victory over Satan in his death, resurrection, and ascension (John 16:32; Eph. 1:20–23; 4:8; Col. 2:15–16). Our circumstances may look like defeat, but Christ has already won the victory.

Confidence. When we follow Jesus by faith, we share in his victory, because "the Lion of the tribe of Judah . . . has prevailed" (Rev. 5:5). The cross was not defeat but victory, for it was there he triumphed over all his enemies (Col. 2:15). When the enemy attacks us, Jesus says to us, "My grace is sufficient for you, for My strength is made perfect in weakness" (2 Cor. 12:9). We may not have confidence in ourselves, but we can always have confidence in Jesus. He gives us the armor we need plus the shield of faith and the sword of the Spirit, which is the Word of God (Eph. 6:10–20).

> [Be] watchful to this end with all perseverance and supplication for all the saints—and for me, that utterance may be given to me, that I may open my mouth boldly to make known the mystery of the gospel.
>
> Ephesians 6:18–19

87

> Therefore, "*Come out from among them*, and be separate, says the Lord. Do not touch what is unclean, and I will receive you."
>
> 2 CORINTHIANS 6:17

From the beginning of Jewish history, when God called Abraham and Sarah, it was his desire that they be a separated nation. The Lord wanted to bless Israel and through them demonstrate what it meant to worship and serve the true and living God. "I will also give You as a light to the Gentiles, that You should be My salvation to the ends of the earth" (Isa. 49:6). The first two generations in the Promised Land were faithful to the Lord, but the third generation departed from God's law and began to imitate the nations around them (Josh. 24:31; Judg. 2:7). The church in Corinth made the same mistake and began to imitate the society around them, and Paul had to admonish them to return to the Lord.

Come out. In our text, Paul quoted from Isaiah 52:11, the prophet's passionate call to the Jews to leave Babylon and return to their own land. What advantage was it for the Israelites to imitate the Gentiles? None at all! The Lord hates idolatry and has always punished it severely. When we worship and serve only the true and living God, we know that we have his presence with us and that we have access to him at the throne of grace when we need him (2 Cor. 6:16–17). He will treat us as his sons and daughters (v. 18) and compassionately care for us. To be able to share his divine nature (2 Pet. 1:4) and call him "Father" is the greatest privilege possible. To have access into his presence (Rom. 5:2; Heb. 4:14–16) means we can get wisdom from him and obtain the help we need day after day. Read Psalm 115 and rediscover the vast difference between the living God and dead idols.

Stand out. When we imitate the idols of this world, we blend right in with "the crowd," but when we imitate the Lord (Eph. 5:1) we stand out with distinction. The compromising Christian becomes a nobody; his light is hidden (Matt. 5:13–16) and instead of being a voice for God he is an echo of the world. God's method for reaching lost people is not imitation but incarnation. He sent his Son in the likeness of flesh so that he could be seen and heard and eventually be crucified. "Christ lives in me," Paul wrote (Gal. 2:20). That's incarnation! The Holy Spirit enables us to reveal Christ to the world around us and make a difference where we live. "Follow Me," Jesus said, "and I will make you fishers of men" (Matt. 4:19). It is when we are different that we attract others and they wonder what the difference is. Jesus befriended sinners but never imitated their way of life, and yet they were attracted to him and listened to his teaching. The church that imitates the world with hopes of attracting the world will be disappointed. Lost people can tell the difference.

Reach out. We are *in* the world but not *of* the world so that we can reach out and rescue people *from* the world. There were times in the history of Israel when people came from great distances to see "God's kingdom," and some of them turned from their dead idols to trust the living God. Had Israel been like any other nation, this could not happen (*see* 1 Cor. 14:22–25). In his Sermon on the Mount (Matt. 5–7), Jesus describes a lifestyle that is countercultural. He wants us to be different, but not odd. We are "ambassadors for Christ" (2 Cor. 5:18–21) and our uniform is godliness. Are we so like the world that we blend right in and have no impact at all?

> [If] an unbeliever . . . comes in, he is convinced by all; he is convicted by all. And thus the secrets of his heart are revealed; and so, falling down on his face, he will worship God and report that God is truly among you.
>
> 1 Corinthians 14:24–25

88

There is neither Jew nor Greek, there is neither slave nor free, there is neither male nor female; for you are *all one in Christ Jesus.*

GALATIANS 3:28

The Romans were effective organizers. They had places for everybody and made sure that each group and individual stayed in their assigned places. The only place in the Roman Empire where gender, nationality, and social class made absolutely no difference was in the local assemblies of God's people. In each local church there was "one flock and one shepherd" (John 10:16), for they were all one in Christ Jesus. In our Lord's high priestly prayer (John 17), he asked the Father to make us one and the Father granted his request. Christians are not "one" organizationally but spiritually, just as Jesus and the Father are one (vv. 11, 20–23). But our unity must not be an isolated attribute of the churches, for unity must be wedded to other blessings.

Unity must be joined with *diversity*, for unity without diversity is uniformity, and uniformity paralyzes a church. The Spirit has given each of us different gifts and abilities, and this diversity is one of the strengths of the church (Rom. 12; 1 Cor. 12; Eph. 4). Each believer is important to the work of the church, no matter what gifts they may possess. Sameness leads to tameness, but the cultivation of a variety of spiritual gifts leads to vitality and variety. Legalists want "cookie-cutter Christians" who are all like them, but the Lord wants variety in his family.

Unity must be joined with *maturity*, for only a healthy, maturing body can stay strong and be able to serve. This is one reason why 1 Corinthians 13 is sandwiched between chapters 12 and 14, the "body" chapters. Love is the circulatory system of the church, for without love, diversity becomes competition 'and competition brings division (*see* James 4:1–6).

Unity belongs with *ministry*. Just as every member of the human body serves the other members, so believers must use their gifts to serve one another. Get out your Bible concordance and look up the "one another" verses. The church's ministry is to take the gospel message to the whole world, and our unity in Christ helps make this possible. The world hates us (John 17:14), but our love and unity bear witness that we belong to God (vv. 21–22). It was said of the early church, "Behold, how they love one another!" May the lost also say, "Behold, how they love us!"

Unity is also written into our *destiny*. Jesus has given his glory to each believer so that our bodies are his temples (John 17:22; 1 Cor. 6:19–20), but he also prayed that we would behold his glory in heaven (John 17:24). There will be unity in heaven—no denominational banners, no competition, nobody asking, "Who is the greatest? Who gets the credit?" Why? Because all that will matter in heaven is the glory of God. Once we behold his glory, any other glory will be nothing. Which leads to this conclusion: If we shall have love and unity in heaven for eternity, *why can't we start practicing it now?* If we are destined to be together in the land of love and glory, let's get acquainted now and show the world the glorious unity of God's people. Not as one big organization but as one big demonstration on earth of unity and love. We are united *spiritually*, but Jesus wants us to be united *visually* before a divided and competitive watching world. What good is our witness to God's love if they don't see that love in action?

> For this is the message that you heard from the beginning, that we should love one another.
>
> 1 John 3:11

89

> *For we are His workmanship*, created in Christ Jesus for good works, which God prepared beforehand that we should walk in them.

EPHESIANS 2:10

There are no "self-made" people in the church of Jesus Christ, "for it is God who works in you both to will and to do for His good pleasure" (Phil. 2:13). God works in us and through us as individuals, and we then make our ministry contribution to the church. For each of his children, our Father has prepared a life plan that perfectly fits us in every way. He uses several tools as he patiently and lovingly works in and on our lives.

God's Word equips us. "All Scripture is given by inspiration of God, and is profitable for doctrine, for reproof, for correction, for instruction in righteousness, that the man of God may be complete, thoroughly equipped for every good work" (2 Tim. 3:16–17). As we read the Word, study it, meditate on it, and seek to obey it, we find ourselves growing in grace and knowledge and being able to serve the Lord more and better. How did Jesus train his disciples? "For I have given them the words which You have given Me. . . . I have given them Your word" (John 17:8, 14). It isn't enough that we hear sermons and Bible lessons and read Christian books. We must immerse ourselves in the Scriptures and allow the Spirit to teach us (16:12–15).

God's Spirit enables us. We must pray that God would grant us, "according to the riches of His glory, to be strengthened with might through His Spirit in the inner man" (Eph. 3:16) and we must remember that Jesus said, "The spirit indeed is willing, but the flesh is weak" (Matt. 26:41). Just as the Spirit and the Word brought about the old creation, bringing order out of chaos (Gen. 1:1–3), so the Spirit and the Word transform us in the new creation (2 Cor. 5:17). To ignore either one is to experience failure.

God's people encourage us. You and I do not possess all the gifts of the Spirit; therefore, we need each other and must minister to each other. During my many years of ministry, I have learned that no Christian is unneeded and no spiritual gift is unimportant. Because we belong to each other, we affect each other and we need each other. I would like to have been at the church at Antioch when God called Paul and Barnabas to go on the first missionary journey (Acts 13:1–4). The prophets and teachers were ministering to the Lord and fasting when the Spirit called Paul and Barnabas to be missionaries, and the Spirit through the church sent them out (vv. 4–5). During his ministry, Paul was grateful for the churches that prayed for him and helped to support him, and what a privilege it was for the churches to work with him!

God's providence enlarges us. Life is a school, with its ups and downs, problems and mysteries; often we don't even know what the lesson is until we have failed the examination! But God in his providence arranges the experiences of life so that we are challenged to grow and become strong in the Lord. "You have relieved [enlarged] me in my distress," David told the Lord (Ps. 4:1). "He also brought me out into a broad place," David wrote (18:19). When his troubles were enlarged (25:17), David trusted God and found himself being enlarged. God prepares us for what he prepares for us, and he goes before us to help us accomplish his will. We are his workmanship, and our responsibilities are to yield to his powerful hands, trust his perfect will, and obey his loving commands. He will do the rest in us and through us, and we shall glorify the Lord!

> Therefore, if anyone is in Christ, he is a new creation; old things have passed away; behold, all things have become new.
>
> 2 Corinthians 5:17

90

And do not be drunk with wine, in which is dissipation, but *be filled with the Spirit*.

EPHESIANS 5:18

Paul is contrasting a drunken person with a Christian filled with the Spirit. Indeed, wine is a spirit but not *the* Spirit. It is a substitute for the kind of reality we have in Christ, but most of the world prefers to live on substitutes. When they could have Jesus as their Savior and the Spirit as their encourager, they prefer to drink alcohol to excess and temporarily drive away their problems. When the problems return, they are worse.

The Holy Spirit keeps us in touch with the realities we have in Jesus Christ. Just as Jesus glorified the Father as he ministered on earth (John 17:4), so the Holy Spirit glorifies Jesus as we serve him today (16:14). If what I do points to myself or to the ministry I represent rather than pointing to Jesus Christ, then the Spirit is not at work in my life. Some people don't know the difference between being filled with the Spirit and being fooled by the spirits. Guy H. King said that the Holy Spirit loves Jesus so much that he makes a Christian to be like him, wrote a book about him (the Bible), and is getting a bride for him, the church. If I don't see Jesus in the Scriptures, then I had better stop reading and studying and start praying to confess my sins! To meet Jesus in the Law of Moses, the history of Israel, the psalms, prophets, and epistles, as well as the Gospels and Acts, is to mine the riches of the Bible. For this, we need the teaching ministry of the Spirit.

We also need the Spirit's fullness if we would be effective witnesses for Christ (Acts 1:8). The Spirit filled the early believers at Pentecost (2:4) and empowered them to share the gospel and minister to the new believers. A few weeks before, Peter had denied the Lord three times, but now he declared the gospel with power and courage, and three thousand people gave their hearts to Jesus. Read Peter's sermon in Acts 2 and note how the Spirit helped him understand the truth, quote the relevant Scriptures, and apply the message to the hearts of the listeners. The Spirit helped him magnify Jesus Christ. Some of the people said Peter and his associates were drunk, but they were just the opposite!

We need to be filled with the Spirit so we can do our daily tasks to the glory of God. In the dedicated Christian life, there is no such thing as "secular" and "sacred." Whatever we do in the will of God is sacred because we are doing it to glorify Jesus Christ. More than one Christian woman has this sign in her kitchen: "Divine Service Performed Here Daily."

The Holy Spirit helps us when we pray (Rom. 8:26), and we are commanded to pray "in the Holy Spirit" (Jude 20). This means submitting ourselves to the Lord and allowing the Spirit to remind us of promises, people, burdens, and blessings as we speak to the Father in the name of Jesus. It also means stopping, meditating, worshiping, and giving thanks as the Spirit leads.

The Holy Spirit is "the breath of God" in our inner being. Jesus "breathed on them, and said to them, 'Receive the Holy Spirit'" (John 20:22); and the Father has promised to give the Holy Spirit to those who ask him (Luke 11:13). If we present to him a clean vessel, and if our desire is only to glorify Christ, the Father will keep his promise. Just as we breathe in and out all day, so we need to keep looking to the Father for repeated fillings of the Spirit. Don't live on substitutes and don't be fooled by the spirits. The Holy Spirit loves you and wants to be your constant companion and helper.

If we live in the Spirit, let us also walk in the Spirit.

Galatians 5:25

91

Therefore, my beloved, as you have always obeyed, not as in my presence only, but now much more in my absence, *work out your own salvation* with fear and trembling; for it is God who works in you both to will and to do for His good pleasure.

PHILIPPIANS 2:12–13

These words were written to a local congregation to encourage the people to follow the calling God had given each of them as individuals and all of them as a church. While every local church must worship the Lord, witness to the lost, focus on prayer and the Word of God (Acts 6:4), and serve the community in God's name, it must also engage in whatever unique ministries God appoints. In my own years of itinerant ministry, I have visited hundreds of churches in different parts of the world, and I have seen how God has burdened and equipped congregations, families, and individuals for different kinds of ministries that have glorified his name. The verb "work out" simply means "bring to success," as in the working out of a mathematical problem. The Holy Spirit is infinitely original and has called and gifted people for various ministries, and each church must make room for these ventures of faith. If an individual or a group of members is gripped by a vision for a certain ministry, the church must pray about it and see how the Lord is leading.

Paul's admonition not only challenges congregations, but it calls for cooperation between God and his people. The Lord "works in" and we "work out." God "worked in" the hearts and minds of Bazalel and Aholiab, and they "worked out" and built the tabernacle and its furnishings (Exod. 31:1–11). God "worked in" James Hudson Taylor and he "worked out" the ministry of China Inland Mission. The Lord has deigned to humble himself and use human agents to accomplish his divine purposes. We as individuals must so yield to the Lord that he will be able to move our hearts, teach our minds, and control our wills, so that all of our skills are available for his service. Serving the Lord is a gracious privilege and a great responsibility, which is why Paul tells us to serve with fear and trembling. Yes, there is joy in serving Jesus, but this joy must be balanced with a godly fear that motivates us to please him. "Serve the LORD with fear, and rejoice with trembling" (Ps. 2:11). It is very destructive when somebody with an inflated ego tries to begin a ministry without the Lord's guidance and help.

We have looked at the *congregation* being sensitive to God's leading, and at the importance of *cooperation* between believers and the Lord. Now we must look at *commendation*, praising the Lord and giving him all the glory. I have seen well-meaning but misguided believers start works on their own, only to see these so-called ministries crumble and vanish. If God gives birth to a new work and we obey his will, that work will prosper, but if, like Peter and his friends, we go fishing without God's guidance, we will catch nothing until we invite him to take over (John 21:1–14). If God's work is done in God's way for God's glory, he will one day reward his faithful servants at the judgment seat of Christ (Rom. 14:10; 2 Cor. 5:10).

The first word in our text is "therefore," referring to the previous passage (Phil. 2:1–11), the humiliation and exaltation of Jesus Christ. Because he is declared Lord, we must make him Lord of our lives today.

> Every tongue should confess that Jesus Christ is Lord, to the glory of God the Father.
>
> Philippians 2:11

92

> For indeed the gospel was preached to us as well as to them, but the word which they heard did not profit them, *not being mixed with faith* in those who heard it.
>
> HEBREWS 4:2

Have you ever read your Bible and not been moved or heard a biblical sermon that seemed to do you no good? Then our text is for you, because it is only when we "mix faith" with the Word of God that we assimilate God's truth and grow.

God gave the good news to Israel that the land of Canaan belonged to them and that they would one day possess it as their permanent home. God first gave the promise to Abraham (Gen. 12:1; 13:14–18) and then affirmed his promise to Isaac, Jacob, and Moses. When Israel left Egypt, they carried Joseph's coffin with them as a reminder that they would eventually dwell in the Promised Land and be at rest from their slavery and their wandering (Gen. 50:22–26; Exod. 13:19). The book of Hebrews uses this slice of history as an illustration of the spiritual rest and inheritance God's people today have in Jesus Christ (Acts 20:32; Eph. 1:11). Note the stages in this wonderful inheritance experience.

Inheritance begins with promises. When Abraham and Sarah left their home in Ur of the Chaldeans, all they knew was that they were heading for a land that God would show them. They walked by faith as day by day the Lord led them. They disobeyed the Lord and went on a detour to Egypt, where they got into trouble, but the Lord forgave them and got them back on course. But the only piece of property Abraham ever owned in Canaan was a cave in which he buried Sarah and where he himself was buried by his son Isaac.

From generation to generation, God's promise stood firm, just as his promises stand firm today.

Promises must be "mixed with faith." When Israel arrived at Kadesh Barnea, they could have entered the land, conquered the enemy, and claimed their inheritance (Num. 13–14). But of all the people there, only Caleb, Joshua, and Moses had the faith to believe that God would give them victory. When we take God's truth into our hearts, the Spirit gives us the faith to act upon it, but the people were walking by sight and not by faith. "Faith comes by hearing, and hearing by the word of God" (Rom. 10:17). "Without faith it is impossible to please Him" (Heb. 11:6).

Faith must be demonstrated by obedience. Faith is obeying God, in spite of the feelings within us, the circumstances around us, or the consequences before us. "As the body without the spirit is dead, so faith without works is dead also" (James 2:26). We can talk about faith, sing about faith, and even pray about faith, but unless we obey what God says, our faith does nothing. An old gospel song says, "Trust and obey / For there's no other way / To be happy in Jesus / But to trust and obey." Some thirty-eight years later, Joshua and the new generation conquered the land and claimed their inheritance.

"Oh, how great is Your goodness, which You have laid up for those who fear You, which You have prepared for those who trust in You" (Ps. 31:19). Not only has our Father prepared blessings for us, but he has also given us "exceedingly great and precious promises" (2 Pet. 1:4) that are the keys that open the treasury of his grace. The Bible is the bankbook that tells us how rich we are, but unless we mix these promises with faith and obey God, we cannot claim the blessings.

But the just shall live by his faith.

Habakkuk 2:4

93

> *But He gives more grace.* Therefore He says: "God resists the proud, but gives grace to the humble."
>
> ═══════════ JAMES 4:6

James wrote this letter to Christian assemblies that were experiencing many problems that are still in churches today. The rich were embarrassing and exploiting the poor, the churches were disputing and dividing, people were professing to be saved and yet did not show it in their lives, and members were using their tongues destructively. *The Christians were proud and worldly and were not living by the grace of God.* James quoted Proverbs 3:34 as both a warning and a promise: "Surely He scorns the scornful, but gives grace to the humble." James assured them that God could give them *more* grace if only they would seek him and ask.

Grace is an undeserved gift. We cannot buy it or earn it. Grace means "God's Resources Available to Christians Everywhere." Not only are sinners saved by grace (Eph. 2:8–9), but believers live by grace, for his grace is sufficient for our every need (2 Cor. 12:9). Grace is free for the asking because Jesus paid the price on the cross. He became poor that we might share the "riches of His grace" (Eph. 1:7). The recipients of James's letter were depending on their words, their wealth, and their plans to give them success, when what they needed was humility, prayer, faith, and the grace of God. God's throne is a throne of grace (Heb. 4:14–16), and we must humble ourselves before him, confess our sins, tell him our needs, and trust him to answer.

Grace is not only an undeserved gift, but it is *an inexhaustible gift.* "And of His fullness we have all received, and grace for grace" (John 1:16). Twice in his letter to the Ephesians, Paul writes of the "riches of His grace" (1:7; 2:7), which simply means there is sufficient grace for everyone, no matter what the needs may be. Too many professed Christians are like the Jewish people in Jeremiah's day who had forsaken the Lord, "the fountain of living waters, and hewn themselves cisterns—broken cisterns that can hold no water" (Jer. 2:13). They depend only on their own strength and skills and ignore God's wealth of grace. If you asked Paul the secret of his life and ministry, he would reply, "But by the grace of God I am what I am. . . . I labored more abundantly than they all, yet not I, but the grace of God which was with me" (1 Cor. 15:10). It's been my privilege over the years to know many Christian leaders, and each of them confessed their own weakness and their dependence on the grace of God. God's grace never runs out!

God's grace is *an essential gift*. We cannot do without it. Our God is "the God of all grace" (1 Pet. 5:10), whether it's saving grace (Eph. 2:8–10), sanctifying grace (Rom. 5:17), suffering grace (2 Cor. 12:7–9), or any of the other "graces" available at the throne of grace. The Bible is "the word of His grace" (Acts 20:32) and reveals to us the "graces" God has for us. The Holy Spirit is the Spirit of grace (Heb. 10:29) and imparts to us what we need when we need it. When Paul and Silas were in jail in Philippi, God gave them "singing grace," and they witnessed to others who were there and won the jailer and his family to Christ (Acts 16:22–34; Col. 3:16). Believers who fail to depend on God's grace and are secretly proud of their achievements are robbing God of the glory he deserves and robbing themselves of the blessing they could be to others (2 Thess. 1:12). God's grace is not a luxury, it is a necessity. *When ministering here on earth, our Lord depended on the grace of God* (Luke 2:40; Heb. 2:9).

> We then, as workers together with Him also plead with you not to receive the grace of God in vain.
>
> 2 Corinthians 6:1

94

If you call on the Father, who without partiality judges according to each one's work, conduct
yourselves throughout *the time of your stay* here
in fear.

1 PETER 1:17

How do you picture life? Is life for you a battle, a
party, a race, or a puzzle? In a great measure, how
you picture life helps to determine how you live
your life. In our text, the apostle Peter pictures life as a journey and calls God's people "pilgrims" (1 Pet. 1:1; 2:11). A
vagabond has no home, a fugitive is running from home, and
a stranger is away from home, but a pilgrim is heading home.
Both Paul and Peter picture the human body as a tent (2 Cor.
5:1, 4; 2 Pet. 1:13–14) because it is a temporary dwelling place
for the spirit of man, and when the spirit leaves the body,
the body is dead (James 2:26). If you have trusted Christ as
your Savior and Lord, then you are a pilgrim and stranger
in this world and you can enjoy benefits that unsaved people
cannot enjoy.

To begin with, *pilgrims have a special vision*. They have
turned their backs to the world and their faces toward heaven.
Abraham and Sarah were citizens of the great city of Ur, yet
when the Lord appeared to them, they left Ur for the land that
God would show them (Acts 7:1–5; Heb. 11:9–12). The eyes
of the pilgrim are not focused on this world but on the world
to come, and the way they live in this world is governed by
that vision. When Stephen was being stoned, he saw Jesus in
glory in heaven, and this enabled him to pray for his enemies
before he died (Acts 7:54–60). Christians aren't so "heavenly
minded" that they are no earthly good, as Mr. Moody used to
say, but their vision of heaven motivates them to sacrifice and

serve here and now on earth. Our names are written down in heaven (Luke 10:20) because we are children of God and citizens of heaven. Heaven is our eternal home.

Pilgrims have special values that are not the values of this world. We want to make progress in holiness and we have no interest in the "things that are in this world" (1 John 2:15–17). We travel light, unencumbered by the things that would hinder us from reaching our appointed goals (Heb. 12:1–2). During his reign, King David accumulated a large amount of money that he donated to the fund for building the temple. In his prayer, he reminded himself and his people that life is short and we are quickly passing through this world. "For all things come from You, and from Your own we have given You. For we are aliens and pilgrims before You, as were all our fathers; our days on earth are as a shadow, and without hope" (1 Chron. 29:14–15). We live with eternity's values in view. We have an inner journey of the heart that day by day makes us more like the Lord, as we and our fellow believers travel together with him.

Pilgrims experience a special victory. We look forward to the coming of Jesus, but if he doesn't come in our lifetime, we are not afraid to die. When he was introduced to Pharaoh, Jacob described his life as a pilgrimage (Gen. 47:9); and when it came his time to die, he had his pilgrim staff with him and was ready for the journey (Heb. 11:21). Death had no victory over him. God's people are "more than conquerors" (Rom. 8:37). For us, death is victory, not defeat.

It's all a matter of the heart. If your heart is fixed on this world, you are not living like a pilgrim, but if your heart is fixed on Jesus and his promises for the future, your life will tell others that this world is not your home.

How is your heart set?

> Blessed are those whose strength is in you,
> whose hearts are set on pilgrimage.
>
> Psalm 84:5 TNIV

95

[Cast] all your care upon Him, *for He cares for you.*

In spite of what some preachers proclaim, Christians do have cares. They have cares because they are human and live in a fallen world. They care for others and that adds to their burdens. Living a godly life in an ungodly world invites opposition and persecution from the enemy who prowls like a lion looking for prey (1 Pet. 5:8). Some of the finest Christians have been in some of the deepest valleys because of their faithfulness to Christ. When your heart is burdened by a weight of care, once and for all *by faith* commit all your cares to the Lord and meditate on what he is to you.

He is your Creator and cares about his creation. "Therefore let those who suffer according to the will of God commit their souls to Him in doing good, as to a faithful Creator" (4:19). If our Father in heaven can handle the affairs of the universe, can he not also take care of us? When David surveyed God's marvelous creation, he asked, "What is man that You are mindful of him, and the son of man that You visit him?" (Ps. 8:4). From the brightest star to the smallest worm, creation is under God's care—and that includes his children, made in his image. Our Lord pointed out that, if God gave food to the sparrows and beauty to the flowers, would he not meet the needs of his children (Matt. 6:25–34)? Peter himself experienced the care of the Lord many times. He caught a fish with a coin in its mouth and paid his temple tax. Twice he had great catches of fish, and once he even walked on water! The night before he was to be executed, Peter was delivered from prison. We matter to the Lord, and he cares for us.

He is your Redeemer and cares about his children. Peter had been a "witness of the sufferings of Christ" (1 Pet. 5:1) and knew the price Jesus paid to save sinners, "who Himself bore our sins in His own body on the tree" (2:24). If our heavenly Father paid such a great price to save us, why would he not care for us? Paul shows the logic of this: "He who did not spare His own Son, but delivered Him up for us all, how shall He not with Him also freely give us all things?" (Rom. 8:32). If the Father gave his greatest gift to us, why would he withhold the lesser gifts that we need? The cross is the greatest evidence of God's love for us. Christ identified himself with our sufferings to the fullest extent so that he might be able to be our sympathetic high priest and help bear our burdens (Heb. 4:14–16).

He is your King and rules his kingdom with grace and mercy. Whenever we feel that this world is a runaway truck out of control, we need to remember that Jesus Christ is not in the manger, on the cross, or in the tomb. He is seated on the throne of the universe "far above all principality and power and might and dominion, and every name that is named" (Eph. 1:21). He told his disciples, "All authority has been given to Me in heaven and on earth" (Matt. 28:18). If he has all authority then he can help us with all our burdens and work out his perfect will. We must never forget the providence of God and his ability to make "all things work together for good to those who love God, to those who are the called according to His purpose" (Rom. 8:28).

He cares for us. We may not feel it or immediately see what he is doing, but he cares for us. If we humble ourselves before him (1 Pet. 5:5–6) and once and for all commit ourselves into his keeping, in his time he will glorify himself by meeting every need. We have our cares, but God cares for us *and will care for our cares if we let him.*

> You have granted me life and favor,
> And Your care has preserved my spirit.
>
> Job 10:12

96

> Beloved, now are we children of God; and it has not yet been revealed what we shall be, but we know that when He is revealed, *we shall be like Him*, for we shall see Him as He is.

1 JOHN 3:2

J ohn began with *a marvel*, that people like you and me should not only be *called* children of God (1 John 3:1) but actually *be* the children of God. What grace! The children of notorious criminals have sometimes changed their names and moved to other cities because they didn't want to be branded as criminals themselves. But here we have the Lord taking us into his family in spite of the reputation we have as sinners. "But God demonstrates His own love toward us, in that while we were still sinners, Christ died for us" (Rom. 5:8). If we have experienced a new birth through faith in Jesus Christ, then we should be growing in grace and pleasing the Lord in our character and conduct. If we ever lose the wonder of this miracle, we will grieve our Father in heaven and disgrace the family name here on earth. The early church magnified the name of Jesus in the way they lived and the message they preached, and they were told to stop (Acts 4:17–20) but they kept right on glorifying his name. How many family names have been disgraced by the conduct of its members? May the Lord help us honor the name of Jesus!

John continued by discussing *a mystery*: "and it has not yet been revealed what we shall be" (1 John 3:2). When John wrote the book of Revelation, the Lord showed him some of the glories of the new Jerusalem, but we do not know what life will be like in the Father's house (John 14:1–6). To be like Jesus means to have the kind of body he had after his resurrection and now has in heaven. When Jesus returns, he will "transform our lowly body that it may be conformed to His glorious body" (Phil. 3:21). Our Lord lives "according to the power of an endless life" (Heb. 7:16). In heaven, the glorified body will feel no pain, sickness, or death, nor will it shed tears, which is good news for all of us but especially for the many who live with physical suffering or who fight painful emotional battles. The best is yet to come!

Then John used the marvel of what we are and the mystery of what we shall be to generate a *motive in our hearts to become more like Jesus today*. "And everyone who has this hope in Him purifies himself, just as He is pure" (1 John 3:3). If a holy city is our eternal destination, then we ought to become holy people while we are waiting. We don't know when Jesus will return. His return will be "in a moment, in the twinkling of an eye" (1 Cor. 15:52). *How much we enjoy the glories of heaven when we arrive will depend on the preparation we made while on earth*. Every vessel will be filled in heaven, but some vessels will be larger than others. If today we are growing in grace and in the knowledge of Christ and his Word, we will appreciate our new home much more. When you plan to visit a different city or country, you wisely study up on the places you will see so that you will be better prepared to enjoy them. A holy life today will help prepare us to enjoy our heavenly home, and by living a holy life on earth we will help others go to heaven with us.

All who have trusted Jesus as their Lord and Savior have a home in heaven, but those who are surrendered to the Holy Spirit and are becoming more and more like Jesus will have "larger vessels" and will enjoy more of heaven's blessings. Does that motivate you today to be like him? How large is your vessel?

> Watch therefore, for you do not know what hour your Lord is coming.
>
> Matthew 24:42

97

> Beloved, *let us love one another*, for love is of God; and everyone who loves is born of God and knows God.
>
> 1 JOHN 4:7

At least fifteen times in the New Testament we find the phrase "love one another," five of them in 1 John (3:11, 23; 4:7, 11, 12). In his upper room message, Jesus admonished his disciples three times to love one another (John 13:34; 15:12, 17), and he even washed their feet to demonstrate that love. Why? Because as the twelve gathered that evening, they were arguing over which of them was the greatest (Luke 22:24). If love is the greatest virtue we can possess (1 Cor. 13:13), then those who practice love and serve others are the greatest in the kingdom. That settles the argument. "Behold, how they love one another!" people said of the early church, but the church scenario today would probably evoke a cry of, "Behold, how they fight one another!"

Christians have *a command to obey*, but can love be "commanded"? Isn't love a mystical romantic feeling over which we have little or no control? That may be Hollywood's idea of love, but it certainly isn't God's. Jesus has the right to command us to love one another because Christian love is an act of the will. Christian love means *treating others the way God treats us*, and the more we obey, the more our feelings and attitudes also change. I have learned that God loves and blesses people I disagree with, and even people I may not like, but I have also learned that God can help me love these people and perhaps encourage them to love me. In the churches and other ministries where I have served, there have usually been people who were difficult to work with, but I determined with God's help to love them and serve them. Today, some of them are among my friends. We *can* obey the command if we experience God's love.

Christians have *a lesson to learn.* If we were not born selfish and demanding, we would probably die, for a baby's cries and a very young child's rebellion are the only tools they have to let us know their needs. But there comes a time when children must learn to love, and the process isn't easy. Even the Lord has to teach his children to love one another. "But concerning brotherly love you have no need that I should write to you, for you yourselves are taught by God to love one another" (1 Thess. 4:9). God the Father teaches us to love one another by the giving of his own Son to be our Savior. "For God so loved the world that He gave His only begotten Son, that whoever believes in Him should not perish but have everlasting life" (John 3:16). Love sacrifices the best for the good of others. God the Son teaches us to love by his own example of sacrifice and service. "Greater love has no one than this, than to lay down one's life for his friends" (15:13). God the Holy Spirit teaches us to love one another by putting love in our hearts and helping us to share it with others. "Now hope does not disappoint, because the love of God has been poured out in our hearts by the Holy Spirit who was given to us" (Rom. 5:5). If we don't truly love others, it isn't the fault of our teachers.

Christians have *a joy to experience.* The Spirit's maturing of love in our hearts is a source of joy, and that maturing is described in Paul's prayer in Philippians 1:9–11. Take time to read it. Love is the first of the Spirit's fruit, followed by joy and peace (Gal. 5:22). With God's love controlling our hearts, we can face opposition, criticism, hatred, and even threat of death, and be more than conquerors to the glory of God. To love God and love our neighbors fulfills the two greatest commandments, but always remember: "He first loved us" (1 John 4:19).

And this I pray, that your love may abound still more and more in real knowledge and all discernment.

Philippians 1:9 NASB

98

But you, beloved, building yourselves up on your most holy faith, *praying in the Holy Spirit*, keep yourselves in the love of God.

JUDE 20–21

Effective prayer involves a living relationship with the Trinity. We pray to God the Father (Matt. 6:9), in the name of Jesus his Son (John 14:13–14), and "in the Holy Spirit" (Jude 20). The Father is the giver of every good and perfect gift (James 1:17) and has a wealth of blessing stored up for us. But we cannot come to him in our own name. Our Savior has given us permission to use his name when we pray, and what a privilege that is! But this means that we must ask the Father only for that which Jesus himself would ask. This is where "praying in the Holy Spirit" comes in, for the Spirit gives us the power and guidance we need for effective prayer. We must thank the Father for his generosity in answering prayer and thank the Son for giving us his authority to pray. But we must yield to the Holy Spirit who dwells in us if we are to have the spiritual energy and guidance we need to pray in the will of God.

We must follow the Holy Spirit's instructions. These are given to us in the Bible and we must not ignore them, because the Word of God and prayer belong together. "If you abide in Me, and My words abide in you, you will ask what you desire, and it shall be done for you" (John 15:7). How can we pray in God's will if we ignore the promises and precepts of the Lord? The examples of prayer found in Scripture encourage us to trust the Lord to answer, and Scripture itself may be turned into prayer. The prophet Daniel learned from reading the book of Jeremiah that Israel's Babylonian captivity would last seventy years, and he immediately began to pray for the

Lord to fulfill his promises (Dan. 9). God's commands express God's will, so when we turn them into prayer, we know we are praying in the will of God. Many times in my ministry, the Lord has shown me promises in the Scriptures that have encouraged me and enabled me to know just what to do. Have an open Bible and an open heart whenever you pray.

We must depend on the Holy Spirit's intercession. Our Savior intercedes before the Father so we can speak to him (Rom. 8:34; Heb. 7:25) and the Holy Spirit intercedes within our hearts so the Father can speak to us (Rom. 8:26–27). The Spirit knows the will of the Father and the Son and can guide us as we pray. I recall times when I have prayed about certain matters for a week or two and then suddenly realized that the Spirit was not joining me in my request, so I removed it from my prayer notebook. A friend of mine compares the Spirit's intercession to the "autopilot" in an airplane. If for some reason the plane gets off course, the autopilot goes to work and gets the plane back on course.

We must obey the Holy Spirit's impressions in our heart. My wife and I have both had the experience of being awakened at night and impressed to pray for someone, only to learn later that the person was facing a crisis at that time. When I have been praying in my daily devotional time and been impressed to intercede for someone or some ministry, I have learned to interrupt my prayer and obey the Spirit's leading. One day in heaven I will discover what was involved. We must learn to exercise discernment when we receive these impressions lest we are detoured by the spirits instead of directed by the Spirit. If we are lying to the Spirit (Acts 5:3), grieving the Spirit (Eph. 4:30) or quenching the Spirit (1 Thess. 5:19), he will not assist us; but if we are walking in the Spirit (Gal. 5:16), he will not fail us.

The Spirit Himself makes intercession for us.

Romans 8:26

99

The Revelation of Jesus Christ, which God gave Him to show His servants—things which must shortly take place. And He sent and signified it by His angel to His servant John.

REVELATION 1:1

T he name of the last book in the Bible focuses on *history's most important person*. Yes, the book is a prophecy (Rev. 1:3), but at the heart of that prophecy stands Jesus Christ, the Son of God. People study this book in search of prophetic secrets when, first of all, they need to look for Jesus and learn about him. We see him in chapter 1 as the glorified King-Priest. In the next two chapters, he is head of the church, telling the churches their needs and commanding some of the churches to make changes while encouraging the other churches to remain faithful. (What he says applies to churches today.) In chapters 4 and 5, we enter the throne room where the Lamb takes the scroll and begins to wrap up history as he opens the seals. The Lamb becomes the Lion and judgment falls on the world in chapters 6–18. He returns to earth as the Great Conqueror in chapters 19–20, defeating Satan and judging sinners. Chapters 21 and 22 take us into the new Jerusalem where the saints reign with Christ. Hallelujah, what a Savior!

The book of Revelation also describes *history's most important conflict*, a war that has been going on since Satan tempted our first parents. The military conflicts on earth are but public demonstrations of the hidden spiritual conflict going on behind the scenes. John describes this war in contrasting symbols. We see the Lamb opposing the dragon, and the world follows Antichrist, the dragon, while a remnant follows the Lamb. The great prostitute, the city of Babylon, rules the world with its political power, wealth, commerce, and slavery, while the heavenly holy city—the bride of the Lamb—waits for Jesus to descend from heaven and establish his kingdom. It is the pure bridegroom from heaven that is victorious over the system from hell. The world unites against Jesus by submitting to Antichrist, while a remnant of true believers follow the Lamb and even lay down their lives for the testimony of Jesus. It's the age-old struggle of truth versus lies, heaven versus hell, the blind majority versus the godly minority who follows the Son of God—and the remnant wins!

In his book, John gives us history's most important message: *the people of faith are the overcomers*. The church shall win the battle to the glory of God. "For whatever is born of God overcomes the world. And this is the victory that has overcome the world—our faith. Who is he who overcomes the world, but he who believes that Jesus is the Son of God?" (1 John 5:4–5). In the letters to the seven churches, the Lord tells us who these overcomers are and what their rewards will be. The nations and kingdoms "will make war with the Lamb, and the Lamb will overcome them, for He is Lord of lords and King of kings; and those who are with Him are called, chosen, and faithful" (Rev. 17:14). It's tragic the way some churches and their leaders are compromising with the world and capitulating before the devil's crowd, when Jesus has overcome every enemy through his death (Col. 2:13–15), resurrection, ascension, and enthronement in heaven (Eph. 1:19–23).

I think it was Peter Marshall who said, "It is better to fail in a cause you know will succeed than to succeed in a cause you know will fail." The church today may look like prisoners of war, but just wait! One day the Lamb will reveal himself as the Lion and overcome the enemy, and then he shall reign as King of kings and Lord of lords (Rev. 19:16). We shall overcome!

> And I heard, as it were, the voice of a great multitude, as the sound of many waters and as the sound of mighty thunderings, saying, "Alleluia! For the Lord God Omnipotent reigns!"
>
> Rev. 19:6

100

But hold fast what you have till I come.

Before the Lord pours out judgment on a wicked world (Rev. 6–18), he first passes judgment on seven churches in Asia Minor (Rev. 2–3), because divine judgment begins in the house of God (1 Pet. 4:17). Five of these churches had lost something from their Christian life and ministry and would be chastened because of it. The church of Ephesus had lost its passionate love for Jesus and was only going through the motions. G. Campbell Morgan said they had "reputation without reality." The church at Pergamos had lost purity of doctrine and the congregation in Thyatira, though faithful during suffering, had lost the godly people needed to lead and teach their church. Only a remnant of true believers walked in holiness, and the believers in Laodicea had the wrong values and were lukewarm in their relationship with Jesus. Jesus is coming again and every believer will stand before him at the judgment seat of Christ. But first he will give his people opportunity to repair their losses and get ready for this awesome event. How can we hold fast and keep from losing what the Lord has given us?

We must realize that what we hold *is a precious gift from God*. Holy men of God paid a price to write the Bible, and the Bible cost Jesus his life. Down through the centuries, dedicated servants of God were persecuted, imprisoned, and even slain because they translated the Bible, distributed copies of it, or preached from Scripture. Are pastors showing love for God's truth when they fail to study the Bible and instead borrow other preachers' sermons? If we plan fun and games for Sunday school but ignore Scripture, what does that say to the next generation? Do we use worship music that is based on Scripture?

We must also realize that *what we have is necessary for serving God effectively*. The early church focused on prayer and the ministry of the Word (Acts 6:4). How can the Spirit convict the lost if we fail to declare God's truth? Jesus taught his disciples and they in turn taught the people to love Jesus, love one another, and love the lost; because of their loving witness, thousands were swept into the kingdom. I fear that technology and entertainment are more important today in many churches than are the Word of God and prayer. Christians are imitating the culture instead of living countercultural lives. "Nevertheless, when the Son of Man comes, will He really find faith on the earth?" (Luke 18:8).

Consider this: *what we hold today can be lost tomorrow.* Each local church is one generation short of extinction. I wonder how many church members are truly born again? Are we careful in the choosing of leaders and teachers? Do we practice 2 Timothy 2:2? Satan is a counterfeiter, and one of his chief stratagems is to get religious unbelievers into places of leadership in local churches. "Do you not know that a little leaven leavens the whole lump?" (1 Cor. 5:6).

What we have can be protected. We must appreciate the spiritual treasures that we have; magnify the Lord Jesus Christ; preach, teach, and sing the Word of God; train carefully each new generation; win the lost and mentor them; and keep our eyes open for the devil's traps. When leaders sleep, Satan plants counterfeits (Matt. 13:25), and counterfeits destroy churches. It is important that we watch and pray and make certain we are obeying the Spirit of God.

By the grace of God, let's be awake and alert and determined to hold fast what we have!

> Be diligent to present yourself approved to God, a worker who does not need to be ashamed, rightly dividing the word of truth.
>
> 2 Timothy 2:15

Epilogue

He who testifies to these things says, "Surely I
am coming quickly." Amen. *Even so, come, Lord
Jesus.*

REVELATION 22:20

This is the last prayer recorded in Scripture. From Genesis
4:26, when people "began to call on the name of the
LORD," to Revelation 22:20, the Scriptures have recorded
how men and women of faith have called on the Lord and he
has answered. Pilgrims like Abraham and Sarah were identified
by their tent and altar. The tent marked them as sojourners
and the altar as worshipers of the true and living God. It was
at the altar that they offered sacrifices to the Lord, worshiped
him, and prayed. As you read the Bible, you discover all kinds of
people in all kinds of places asking God to grant them all sorts
of blessings. Isaac prayed that his wife would conceive (Gen.
25:21–26) and Jacob that his brother Esau would accept him
(32:9–32). How many times Moses had to pray, not so much
for himself but for the erring Israelites! Were it not for Moses's
intercession, God might have destroyed the whole nation. Jeremiah was a man of prayer and so was Daniel, and Nehemiah
prayed often during the rebuilding of Jerusalem's walls. Jesus
prayed and so did the apostles, especially Paul. The men and
women of prayer we meet in the Bible bear witness to us that
prayer is not a luxury but a necessity.

When the prayer of Revelation 22:20 is answered at the
return of Christ for his church, it will mark the end of our

ministry of prayer, for I find no references in Scripture that say we will continue to pray when we have our glorified bodies in heaven. In this text, we are asking Jesus to come for us, while today Jesus is asking people to come to him. The word *come* is at the heart of this brief prayer. Jesus invites the weary to come to him for rest (Matt. 11:28–30) and the hungry and thirsty to come to him for food and drink (John 6:35; 7:37–39).

But if we are praying this prayer, *are we sure that we are truly ready for him to come?* Frequently in his parables, the Lord warned his listeners to be prepared for his return. "Let your waist be girded and your lamps burning. . . . Blessed are those servants whom the master, when he comes, will find watching. . . . Therefore you also be ready, for the Son of Man is coming at an hour you do not expect" (Luke 12:35, 37, 40). A friend of mine was convinced that certain great events had to occur before Jesus would return. We were together at a conference and I asked him, "Do you think Jesus could return today?" His emphatic reply was, "No!" I said, "Then you had better get ready, because he said he would come at an hour when you didn't expect him."

The expectation of the imminent return of Christ ought to motivate us to be ready when he comes. Jesus says, "Behold, I am coming as a thief. Blessed is he who watches, and keeps his garments, lest he walk naked and they see his shame" (Rev. 16:15). "And now, little children, abide in Him, that when He appears, we may have confidence and not be ashamed before Him at His coming" (1 John 2:28). The picture in the word *ashamed* is of a servant shrinking back in shame when his master catches him and exposes his disobedience. It suggests that some believers will be ashamed to meet Jesus when he comes.

Praying faithfully for his return will help us be prepared.

And behold, I am coming quickly, and My reward is with Me, to give to every one according to his work.

Revelation 22:12

Warren W. Wiersbe has served as a pastor, radio Bible teacher, and seminary instructor and is the author of more than 160 books, including the popular BE series of Bible expositions. He pastored the Moody Church in Chicago and also ministered with Back to the Bible Broadcast for ten years, five of them as Bible teacher and general director. His conference ministry has taken him to many countries. He and his wife, Betty, make their home in Lincoln, Nebraska, where he continues his writing ministry.